HOW CHARTS CAN HELP YOU IN THE STOCK MARKET

OTHER STANDARD & POOR'S BOOKS

THE STANDARD & POOR'S GUIDE TO LONG-TERM INVESTING
by Joseph Tigue

THE STANDARD & POOR'S GUIDE TO SAVING AND INVESTING FOR COLLEGE
by David Braverman

THE STANDARD & POOR'S GUIDE FOR THE NEW INVESTOR
by Nilus Mattive

Standard & Poor's

HOW CHARTS CAN HELP YOU IN THE STOCK MARKET

William L. Jiler

McGraw-Hill

New York Chicago San Francisco Lisbon London Madrid Mexico City Milan New Delhi San Juan Seoul Singapore Sydney Toronto

The McGraw-Hill Companies

Copyright © 2004, 1962 by The McGraw-Hill Companies, Inc. All rights reserved. Printed in the United States of America. Except as permitted under the United States Copyright Act of 1976, no part of this publication may be reproduced or distributed in any form or by any means, or stored in a data base or retrieval system, without the prior written permission of the publisher.

1 2 3 4 5 6 7 8 9 0 DOC/DOC 0 9 8 7 6 5 4 3

ISBN 0-07-142684-1

Previously published in 1990 by Fraser Publishing Company.

Printed and bound by RR Donnelley.

This publication is designed to provide accurate and authoritative information in regard to the subject matter covered. It is sold with the understanding that neither the author nor the publisher is engaged in rendering legal, accounting, or other professional service. If legal advice or other expert assistance is required, the services of a competent professional person should be sought.

—*From a Declaration of Principles jointly adopted by a Committee of the American Bar Association and a Committee of Publishers*

McGraw-Hill books are available at special quantity discounts to use as premiums and sales promotions, or for use in corporate training programs. For more information, please write to the Director of Special Sales, Professional Publishing, McGraw-Hill, Two Penn Plaza, New York, NY 10121-2298. Or contact your local bookstore.

This book is printed on recycled, acid-free paper containing a minimum of 50% recycled, de-inked fiber.

To predict the course of the stock market, Wall Streeters have tried everything from the height of tides to the frequency of sunspots. The most practical tools are charts that show the price changes of individual stocks as well as the action of the market as a whole. Chartists are powers in the Street; on what their charts show, institutions, mutual funds and thousands of individual investors buy and sell.
—Time *magazine.*

ACKNOWLEDGEMENTS *This book was years in the making and is the fruit of the labor of many people. Chart ideas and formations had to be carefully researched. Among the hundreds of patterns studied, only a small percentage were finally adopted for use in the book. Reams of written material on charting techniques which were submitted to the author were parboiled, condensed and leached in an attempt to simplify and clarify a most difficult subject.*

The author is especially indebted to Charles Hatten, *a professional investment advisor and chartist for over 25 years, who spent tireless hours on research and writing. He originated the chapter on "The Measured Move" and wrote parts of several other chapters. Considerable editorial assistance was provided by* John Hess, *the well known financial writer.*

The author also gratefully acknowledges research and editorial help from such able market experts as Stephen Greenberg, *H. Hentz & Co.;* Richard D. Donchian, *Director of Commodity Research for Hayden, Stone & Co., Inc.;*

Fred Barton, *of the Commodity Department of Thomson & McKinnon;* Edward Underwood, *of Bache & Co., Inc.;* Harry Jiler, *President of Commodity Research Bureau, Inc.;* Joseph R. Karp, *Investment Advisor; and the late* Lester Wyetzner *of Meller & Company.*

The help and encouragement of Joseph Granville, *author of two popular books on technical stock market analysis and* Kenneth Ward, *Senior Vice-President of Hayden, Stone & Co., Inc., were deeply appreciated.*

The author also wishes to thank Joseph Kesselman *who contributed greatly to the production of this book, and the chart staff of Trendline who prepared the art work for publication.*

WILLIAM L. JILER

CONTENTS

The illustrations in this book are divided into two categories: (a) simple figures, arbitrarily drawn to show the general appearance of the different formations discussed in the text, and (b) charts for selected listed stocks whose actual fluctuations in the market formed patterns that could be clearly identified.

The charts of listed stocks (without the author's added "pattern identifying" outlines) appeared originally in the stock market chart publications of Trendline.

Trendline, a unit of Standard & Poor's, a division of The McGraw-Hill Companies, Inc., continues to publish clear, informative charts on individual stocks and market indicators using the latest computer and graphics technology.

Its publications include:
DAILY ACTION STOCK CHARTS—A weekly publication that includes 12 month charts of daily price and volume data, moving averages, relative strength and financial statistics on 760 companies accounting for over 85% of the volume on the NYSE. Includes most options stocks.

CURRENT MARKET PERSPECTIVES—A monthly publication that includes 4 year charts of weekly prices and volumes, performance rankings, relative strength, 30 week moving averages and financial data on 2,370 listed and Nasdaq companies.

For more information please write to:

Standard & Poor's/Trendline, Publisher
55 Water Street
New York, NY 10041

or call 1(800) 852-1641.

PLATES

FOREWORD

If you have money in the markets, you have money at risk. This classic book is for anyone who wants to reduce the risks inherent in exposure to the financial markets.

Fundamental analysis is only one part of the equation for stock market success. The most pristine balance sheet in the world, the most consistent year over year or quarter over quarter expansion in revenues or profits do not mean anything if other people are not willing to pay more for a stock than you did. The breakdown in Enron's chart occurred long before the depth of the financial chicanery was fully uncovered.

Do you know what to look for in the charts of companies you own? Without knowledge of price patterns and volume, market participants expose themselves to even higher risks than are necessary to earn a return.

"Buy and hold" works great in a bull market, but bull markets in stocks and stock markets do not last forever. Claiming to be a "long-term investor," or a "buy and holder," is no excuse for ignorance of how charts can help you in the markets. Charts are not just for traders; any long-term investor can benefit by recognizing the patterns illustrated and explained in this book. A long-term time horizon is easily accommodated by simply using longer periods of time in the bars on the charts; weekly or monthly bar charts can be substituted for daily bar charts. The internet is awash with free sites to access stock charts, but what good are free sites if you don't know what to look for?

Charts offer a unique insight into the mind-set of the marketplace. A company's fundamentals usually look their best at the top, but what are the clues inherent in the price and volume action of a stock which can indicate that the institutions are forming an orderly procession for the exits? This book offers you time-proven observations which can help you see the footprints in the snow and reduce the odds of making a "buy and hold forever" mistake.

A technical assessment of price and volume action is an essential tool when putting money at risk in the markets. *How Charts Can Help You in the Stock Market* by William Jiler was first copyrighted in 1962. It has withstood the test of time.

Jiler wastes no one's time. He identifies the most important price patterns and gives clear examples to illustrate his points. He puts a face to the charts; the explanations he gives for the price patterns combined with volume observations allow you to understand the psychology of the marketplace. And he does it in a succinct and direct manner.

This book has been in my stock market library for years. We hope it becomes a permanent fixture in your library as well.

Paul Cherney
Chief Market Analyst
Standard & Poor's
October 2003

HOW CHARTS CAN HELP YOU IN THE STOCK MARKET

1

A TOOL FOR INVESTORS

What makes one stock sell at $50 a share and another at $100?

And what makes the market pay $50 a share for stock at one time—and $100 at another?

Well, there are a company's earnings, dividends, net worth, the outlook for its future business, the outlook for the economy as a whole, the general behavior of the stock market . . . countless factors.

If a diligent investor could learn them all, and balance them properly, he should be able to predict the price of a stock—or so it would seem. Yet, assuming he had a pretty accurate idea of how the earnings of International Business Machines would rise over the last decade, *how could he anticipate that I.B.M. would sell as low as 12 times its annual profit in the late Nineteen Forties and at 60 times earnings in the late Fifties?*

Obviously, "investors' confidence" went up sharply in the Fifties. And obviously, the psychology of the market —that is, the sum of the attitudes of all potential buyers and sellers—is a crucial factor determining prices. It's no use being "right" about a stock, if the market is "wrong." How often does the market go *down* following an announcement of good news, and *up* when the outlook seems dark! Put another way, "a stock is worth only what investors are willing to pay for it."

Thus, to predict the action of a stock, it would be ideal to have all the hard, economic facts, plus an accurate insight into the minds of the public. That recalls the sad old jest, "If I had some ham, I'd fix me some ham and eggs, if I had some eggs." The fact is, nobody can know everything that may affect the price of a stock—not even the vaunted "insider." To be sure, it's an enormous advantage to have advance knowledge about earnings, dividends, stock splits, mergers, oil discoveries or new products. But to profit by such knowledge, the insider—and his sisters and his cousins and his aunts—must buy stock. In so doing, he increases the *demand* for the stock, just as when he is ready to sell, he increases the *supply*. In either case, his action must register itself in the marketplace, where the alert investor may observe the signal.

Now while, as we have just noted, nobody can learn all the factors that may determine the price of a stock, in the last analysis *all* these factors meet in the market and affect the interplay of supply and demand, which *does set* the price. No matter what the news may be concerning a company, *it will affect the price of its stock only when it tips the scale in favor of either supply or demand.* If, at a given point, the demand for a stock (orders to buy) is greater than the supply (orders to sell), the price must go up. If supply exceeds demand, the price must go down.

Charts provide a record of this interplay of supply and demand—a history at-a-glance of the trading in a stock, or group of stocks, showing how many shares were traded, at what price and when.

The purpose of "chart reading" or "chart analysis" is to determine the probable strength of demand versus pressure of supply at various price levels, and *thus to predict the probable direction in which a stock will move, and where it will probably stop.*

The clues are provided by the history of a stock's price movements, as recorded on a chart. In the market, history does repeat itself—often. On the charts, price fluctuations tend, with remarkable consistency, to fall into a number of patterns, each of which signifies a relationship between buying and selling pressures. Some patterns, or "formations," indicate that demand is greater than supply, others suggest that supply is greater than demand, and still others imply that they are likely to remain in balance for some time.

Before going any further, let us be clear and emphatic about this: THERE IS NO INFALLIBLE SYSTEM FOR PREDICTING STOCK PRICES. If there were, the inventor of the system would eventually own all the stock in the market. Rather than being infallible, charts are often misleading or misunderstood—so much so, that we try to point this out throughout this book and we also have included a chapter on the pitfalls of chart reading at the end of this book.

Fortunately, it's not necessary to be right all of the time to make money in the stock market. It's only necessary to be right more often than you are wrong. This principle is well known to gamblers, who say "the house never loses." Actually, the house often loses—at least often enough to keep the customers coming back—but that mathematical edge assures that the house will win in the long run. How can one find such an edge in the stock market? Certainly, sound, thorough information about a company, its industry and the economy are valuable. But a knowledge of the stock's chart action, and a familiarity with chart patterns, will help the investor decide when to buy and when to sell.

Now, a look at how the chart is made. (Experienced chart readers may skip the rest of this chapter, but we'd be delighted to have them stay along.) The charts used in this book—and most widely used in price forecasting—are called Vertical Line Charts, the kind that newspapers use to depict the stock averages. There are many other kinds and variations—composed of lines, bars, steps or other symbols, plotted on logarithmic, square root or arithmetic scale. Some analysts use oscillators, moving averages, ratios or "points and figures." Each of these has its merits and its function, but all take a lot of time to keep up, and their interpretation is generally highly complicated.

By contrast, the Vertical Line Chart may easily be kept and understood by anybody, in a minimum of time. It presents at a glance the most pertinent information—the highest, lowest and closing prices and the number of shares traded in a given period. It is also the most time-tested method, having grown in use since the turn of the century. Vertical Line Charts showing the course of leading stocks and market averages for many years are available to the investor through various chart publications. They provide ready-made, up-to-date charts of leading stocks, and he can easily build and maintain his own charts for the stocks he is interested in.

The chart is built to show either daily, weekly, monthly or even yearly price fluctuations. The same patterns can be recognized in any of these, and they may be used with equal effect in forecasting—but the daily chart will often signal a turn more quickly, and so most of the illustrations in this book are daily charts. Weekly and monthly ones are handy, however, for studying long-range trends, and examples appear at the end of the chapters that follow.

In any case, the price information is entered on graph paper of the ordinary kind, with even horizontal and vertical rules. The up-and-down scale, printed on the sides, measures prices; the scale along the top or bottom indicates the time it happened—the day, week, month or year, as the case may be. From the stock market table, as published in the newspapers, or reported on the ticker, the chart-maker enters a dot to mark the highest price at which the stock was traded that day, and another dot to mark the low. A vertical line drawn between these dots shows the price range for the day. A short, thin crossline will mark the price of the last transaction of the day. For example, a stock that was traded Oct. 15 at prices ranging from $45 to $47 a share, with the last trade at $46, will appear as follows:

FIGURE 1

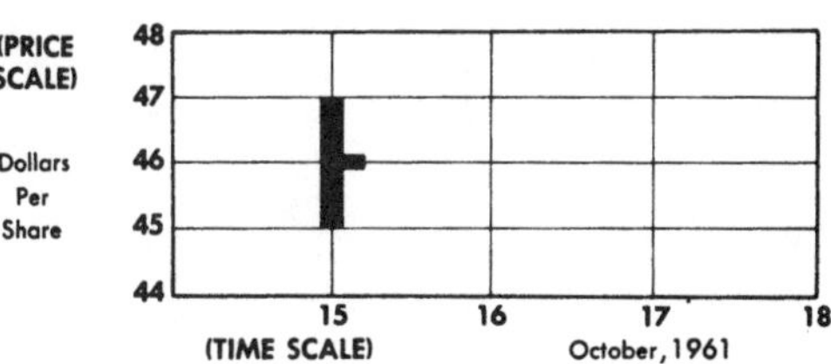

Weekly, monthly or yearly charts are, of course, drawn in the same way, with each line corresponding to the price action for such a period.

Space is provided at the bottom of the chart to add an important piece of information: the number of shares (or volume) traded during each period. This is recorded as a vertical bar extending up from zero to the correct figure, in accordance with a scale along the side. (In newspaper market tables, the volume is given in hundreds of shares, or "round lots," unless otherwise indicated.)

The convenience—indeed the necessity—of charts may now be seen by considering the daily market action of General Motors stock from Sept. 15 to Oct. 15, 1961, first on a table of figures—

FIGURE 2 GENERAL MOTORS

Date	High	Low	Close	No. of shares Traded
Sept. '61				
15	48	47¼	48	37,100
16	Sat.			
17	Sun.			
18	48	47	48	38,200
19	48	47⅜	47⅜	28,500
20	48⅛	47⅜	48⅛	36,300
21	49	48¼	48½	59,700
22	48¾	48¼	48⅝	29,500
23	Sat.			
24	Sun.			
25	49	48	48¼	44,100
26	48¾	48¼	48½	29,500
27	49¾	48½	49¾	75,700
28	49⅞	49½	49⅝	48,200
29	49¾	49¼	49⅝	31,800
30	Sat.			

Oct. 1	Sun.			
2	49¾	49¼	49¾	29,200
3	49¾	49⅜	49⅝	21,500
4	50	49⅜	50	55,200
5	50⅜	50	50⅜	45,800
6	50¾	50¼	50⅝	41,100
7	Sat.			
8	Sun.			
9	50⅞	50⅜	50¾	37,100
10	51	50⅝	50¾	40,000
11	51	50⅝	51	35,300
12	50⅞	50⅜	50⅜	26,400
13	50⅛	49¾	50⅛	39,300
14	Sat.			
15	Sun.			

And then on a chart—

FIGURE 3

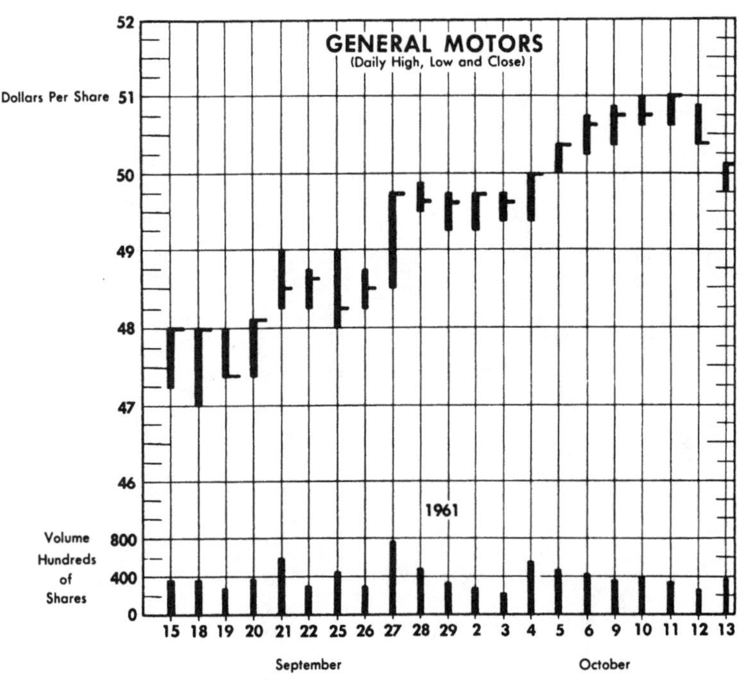

The first vertical line shows that, on Sept. 15, prices paid for G.M. ranged from a high of 48 to a low of 47¼, closing at 48 (horizontal dash); the line at the bottom shows that 37,100 shares of G.M. were traded that day.

The same procedure was followed for each day through Oct. 15. (It will be noted that space for week-ends is eliminated to provide continuity.)

These data may be condensed, for the purpose of examining long-term trends, into a weekly range chart, as follows:

FIGURE 4

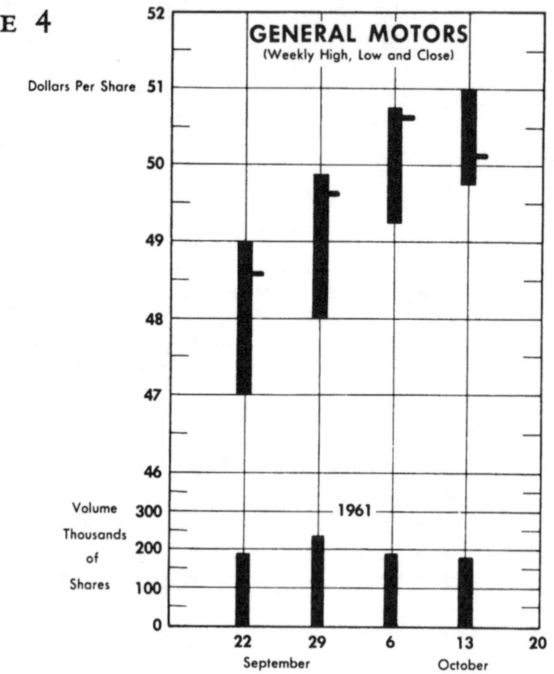

TRENDS

A mere glance at a few stock charts will reveal that prices have a prevailing tendency to move in a particular direction for a considerable time. A closer examination will show that this tendency, or *trend,* frequently assumes a definite pattern, zig-zagging along an imaginary straight line. *In fact, this ability of prices to cling extremely close to a straight line is one of the most extraordinary characteristics of chart movements.*

Now, there is nothing mystical or hocus-pocus about chart reading. Stocks trace various patterns for reasons soundly based in human psychology—and it's psychology that determines stock movements. The tendency of stocks to move along a straight line, for example, is not hard to explain. In physical terms, it often is likened to the law of inertia; that an object in motion will continue in motion in the same direction, until it meets an opposing force. In human terms, an investor will tend to resist paying more for a stock than the price other people have recently been paying for it—unless it continues moving up, which will give him some confidence or hope that it will keep going up. Conversely, an investor will resist selling a stock for less than the price other people have been getting for theirs—unless the price keeps declining, and he fears it will continue to decline.

Let us see how market psychology, reacting to a news development, forms a trend in an imaginary, but highly typical, case. Suppose the XYZ Corporation is nearing completion of the development of a new product that promises to increase sales and earnings. Its stock has been selling at $20 a share. Insiders—executives, employees, relatives and friends—are the first to learn about it. They are immediately removed from the ranks of those who might be willing to sell their stock at $20, $21 or even $22. Their shares are off the market, and to that extent, the supply of stock at those prices has been reduced, creating a tendency for the stock to rise. More important, some of them will begin to buy more stock, increasing the demand. By this time, word of the new product may have reached brokers, investment counselors and perhaps other people in the industry concerned. The price has been rising steadily, to $23, $24, $25, attracting more and more attention, and traders and the general public begin to scramble aboard. Everybody loves to give or get a stock tip (this is one of those rare ones that are sound) and more and more buyers are attracted.

Then comes the public announcement of the new product. Brokerage firms, in pamphlets sent to their clients, discuss what effect it will have on XYZ's earnings. XYZ itself advertises and publicizes the item. All this creates new demand. But there comes a point when the market price has fully "discounted" the development—that is, the stock has risen enough to take into account the increase in earnings likely to occur. This point is often reached by the time the public announcement is made. Many traders "sell on the news" to cash in their profits, especially when the news occurs after a sharp price rise.

A downtrend may develop if it appears that the rise went too far. Perhaps the early estimates of sales and earnings were too optimistic. Perhaps other companies quickly introduce competitive products. Or profits from other XYZ departments may decline. As the price of XYZ falls back, buyers who still have profits may cash in. Then, latecomers who bought near the top of the rise may, in disgust, sell out at a loss, to avoid even bigger losses. And so the decline continues.

So, for such well-founded reasons, stock prices do tend to move in a given direction for a considerable time—up, down or "sideways." Thus, an obvious first lesson to be drawn from chart reading is that, when a stock is found to be following a given trend line, *it is more likely to continue moving along that line than not to.* Not certain, just likely. But the ability to spot a trend gives the investor an edge in determining his market tactics.

HOW TO SPOT A TREND

In the course of a stock's normal wavy movement across the chart, as few as three points, each marking the top or bottom of a wave, may suggest the presence of a trendline; more are usually needed to confirm it. In Figure 5, note that in the uptrend, the third point, C, becomes fixed at a higher level than the first point, A. With only three points observed so far, the trendline may be difficult to recognize until prices move away from Point C and in some cases actually cross Point B. In the downtrend, Point C is lower than Point A. "Sideways," or horizontal trendlines may occur when Point C is even with Point A.

FIGURE 5

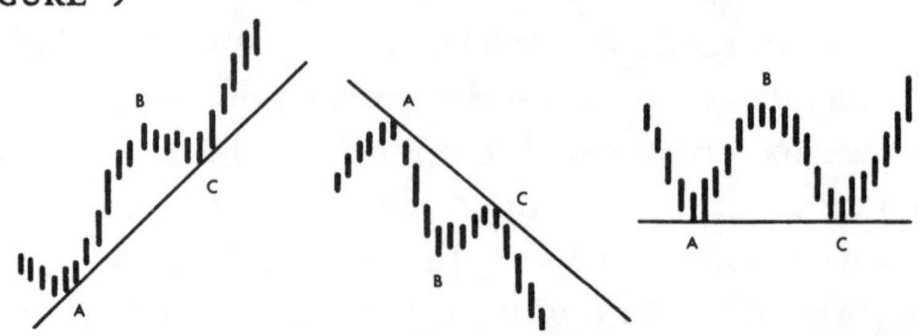

UPTREND LINE DOWNTREND LINE SIDEWAYS TRENDLINE

Please note that the *up*trend line is drawn by connecting the *lower* points of a stock movement. A *down*trend line must be drawn by connecting the *higher* points. This is an important distinction. The inexperienced chart reader invariably—and quite naturally—does the opposite, drawing uptrends from the upper limits and downtrends from the lower ones. This technique appears to work at times, but experience has shown it to be highly unreliable and of little use in precise forecasting, where it is desired to determine at what point a stock is likely to halt on its next swing. When a sideways trend forms, both upper and lower points often conform to parallel, straight horizontal lines, but it is safer to draw a sideways trendline along the low points, as one does for a hypothetical uptrend.

Figure 6 (page 31) shows how trendlines and channels would look on a daily basis vertical line chart. How trendlines actually develop are shown in the charts at the end of this chapter, all taken from actual market action. The heavy, solid lines are the trendlines. The broken lines, which were drawn parallel to the trendlines, help to outline *channels*. Briefly, channels are grooves or ducts through which prices move as they zigzag along a trendline. Once a trendline has been clearly established, a channel can usually be determined. Needless to say, channels seldom occur as neatly defined as in the selected charts shown in Figure 6, but when found, they are useful in suggesting at what price to buy or sell, if the decision to buy or sell has been made.

FIGURE 6

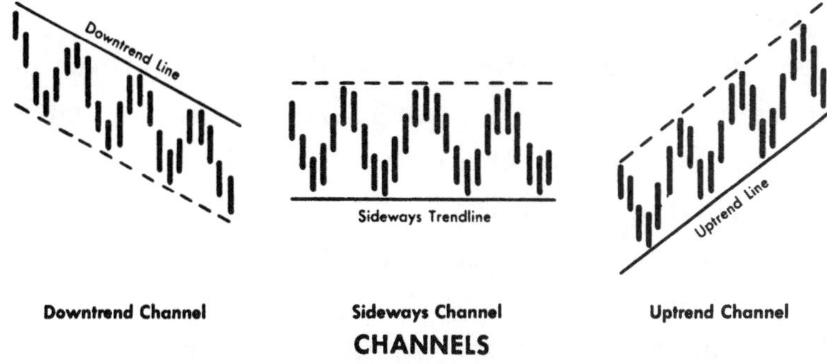

CHANNELS

It is perhaps obvious that the longer a stock has been moving along a given trend, or within a given channel or groove, the stronger that trend is likely to be. For this reason, trendlines on longer range charts such as weekly or monthly high-low-and-close charts are usually more reliable than trendlines that form on daily high-low-and-close charts. Trendlines that form in just a few weeks cannot be expected to hold in the majority of instances. But, even when stocks break away from an established line, and signal a true shift in direction, they have a tendency to return to it. This magnetic attraction of the old trend, this "pull-back effect" common to trendlines, will be observed on the completion of many of the formations covered in later chapters. An awareness of this movement can help the timing of purchases and sales.

FIGURE 7

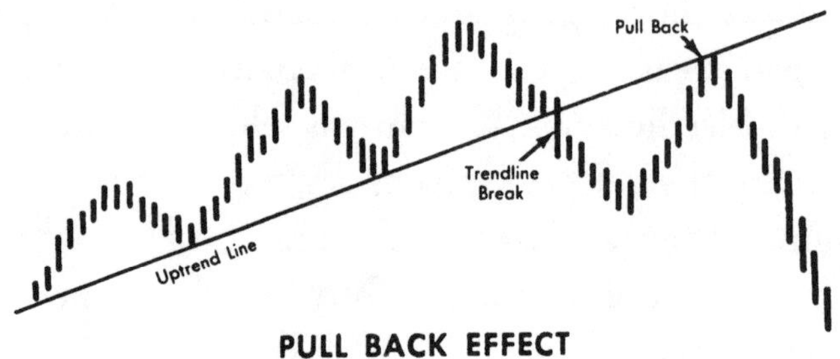

PULL BACK EFFECT

VOLUME

As we have noted, when the analyst sees a three-point formation A-B-C as in Figure 5, he will draw a tentative trendline. This is not yet a signal for action; he must look for confirmation. As time goes on, his chart may be strewn with tentative lines that have been discarded. But he will also find trends that follow through. One of his most important guides will be the volume, or number of shares traded each day. The volume is a measure of the intensity of buying and selling pressure—the *conviction* behind a move. Obviously, if a stock that is seldom traded jumps 5 points on a single trade of 100 shares, the price increase only means that one individual, for reasons best known to himself, wanted 100 shares, and there were none to be had immediately except at a level 5 points "above the market," where some other individual had told his broker he would be willing to sell.

By the same token, the greater the volume, the greater the significance of a price movement, in general. During a normal uptrend, volume increases when prices are rising from the trendline, and volume subsides when prices are falling back to the trendline. Conversely, in a downtrend, the volume is usually greater when prices are falling than when they are rallying.

SHARP TURN AHEAD

Changes in this volume pattern often warn of a reversal in trend before it actually happens. For example, if an uptrend has been proceeding normally, with higher volume on rallies and lower volume on reactions, and *suddenly volume subsides on the rallies and increases on the reactions, it may be a signal of a pending price reversal.*

To the chartist, each break of an established trendline is a caution signal. A single, simple break of a trendline in most cases may not indicate the end of the trend. But it's a warning. And long experience in chart analysis has developed this rule of thumb: *A trend reversal is quite likely to be in process whenever a stock price has broken through its well established trendline by as much as 3 percent, on increased volume.*

VARIATIONS

An interesting variation from the straight-line trend is the curved trendline. In some cases, the momentum of an advance or a decline suddenly picks up steam so rapidly that an established straight trendline curves in the direction of the move. (The activity in XYZ Corporation, described earlier in this chapter, might well produce an accelerating curve.) Figure 8 shows upcurving and downcurving trendlines. If this curving occurs *after an extended price move, it frequently results in a climactic action that brings the major movement to its final peak* (or bottom in a sell-off). Climactic action is synonymous with frenzied buying or selling. Price moves are exceptionally wide and volume is abnormally high. This type of trendline can be drawn with a "French Curve"* and can be just as valid as the straight-line variety. Warning: It is very difficult to pinpoint the end of a climactic move until the reaction phase has begun. The "blow-off" or the vertically rising stage can carry a considerable distance.

FIGURE 8

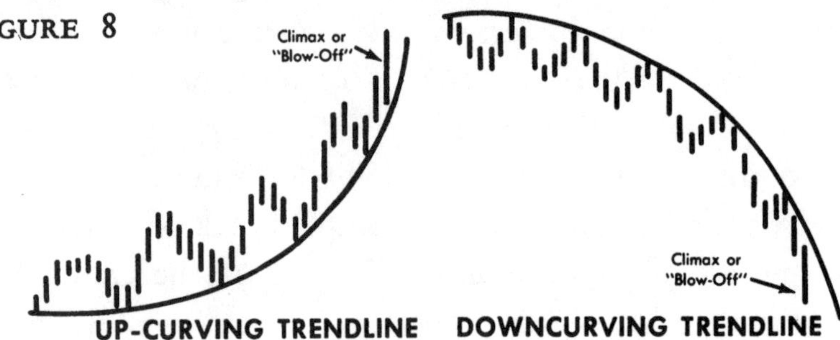

Study will reveal many other variations and complex formations of trendlines. Two interesting variations are the "internal trendline" and the "fan."

Figure 9 shows how an internal trendline forms. The section from A to B is a normal uptrend line, while B to C, forming *beneath* the trendline, makes it an internal line.

FIGURE 9

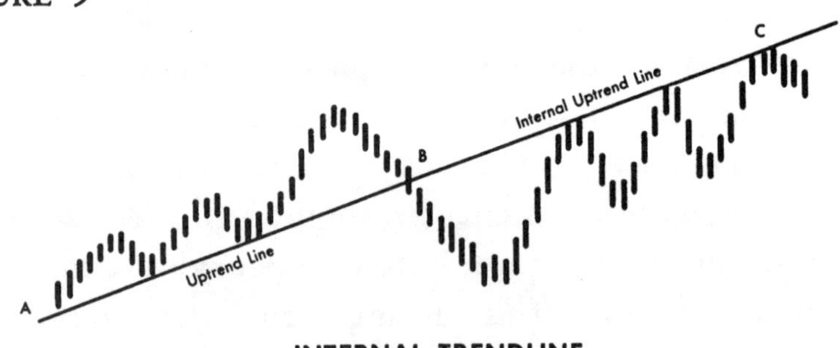

*French Curve—Draftsman's instrument for tracing various curved lines.

A fan (as shown in Figure 10) develops when a well established trendline (A to B) is broken, but prices continue to move in the same direction and soon develop a second trendline (A to C); this second line is broken again, and a third trendline (A to D) forms—still in the same direction. When a third line breaks, *a major turn in trend usually follows.* Sometimes, to be sure, this procedure repeats itself a fourth or even a fifth time—but the odds are overwhelming that a fourth break in a trendline will result in a turnaround.

FIGURE 10

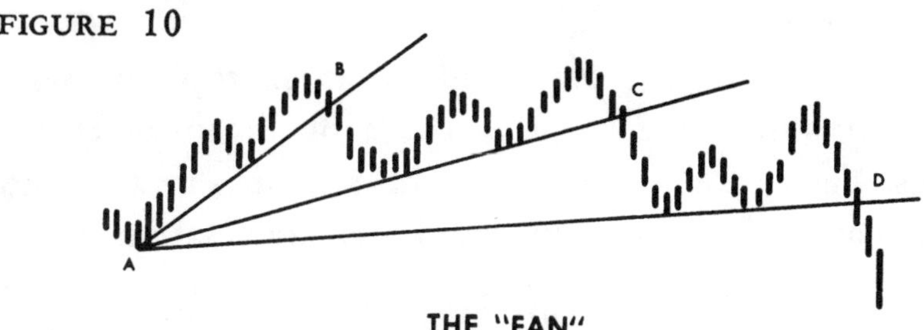

THE "FAN"

MARKET TACTICS

Like a traffic light, the chart advises the knowledgeable investor when to go ahead, slow down or stop. As long as an established upward trendline is intact, the traffic signal is *bright green.* New stock purchases can be made and previous investments should be held. Any break in a trendline flashes the *amber caution* light, especially if the break is on increased volume. New purchases should be deferred, and existing stockholdings should be re-examined. The longer the trendline has held, the more significant will be the eventual breaking of this line as a "bear" signal. Finally, evidence that a downtrend is developing flashes the *red* light, indicating that it's time to sell and cash in on profits, or take other defensive measures to avoid losses. (Brokers are familiar with such defensive steps as selling short "against the box," and buying "puts and calls," which need not be discussed here.)

Assuming that one has decided to buy or sell a stock, he may gain an advantage of as much as several dollars a share by being familiar with the trend channel through which the stock has been fluctuating. He would *buy at the bottom* of the channel, and *sell at the top*. And of course, the *break* of a trendline or the *return move* to a trendline may represent highly favorable buying or selling opportunities.

To "buy at the bottom and sell at the top" of major price moves is of course the unattainable dream of all investors. To try for the last eighth of a point is unwise, and unnecessary. The investor should use imagination at all times, and avoid being bound by hard and fast rules, or fascinated by a formula that offers too precise a forecast of prices. But the trendline is the first and most significant picture to be looked for in any systematic approach to chart reading.

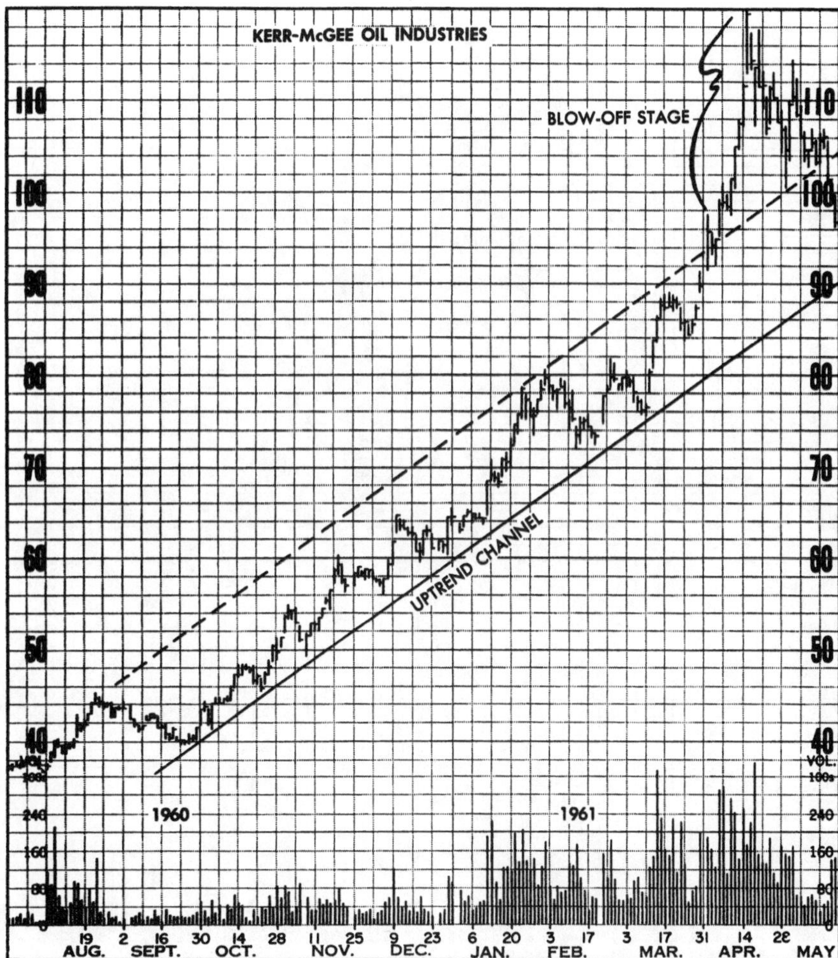

PLATE 1 KERR-McGEE — Uptrend Line and Channel

The chart above shows how Kerr-McGee Oil tripled in value in less than seven months. For the first six months, prices adhered remarkably close to an imaginary uptrend line (heavy line) and within the confines of a relatively narrow channel (outlined by the dotted line drawn parallel to trendline). Further examination will reveal that the trendline was well established within the first month of the advance. In April, 1961, prices broke through the upside of the channel and accelerated into a blow-off or climax phase of development. This type of action often marks a temporary or major top. The vertical part of the rise was attributed to anticipation of a 2 for 1 stock split, which became effective May 31. By early 1962, prices were still well below the highs recorded on this chart.

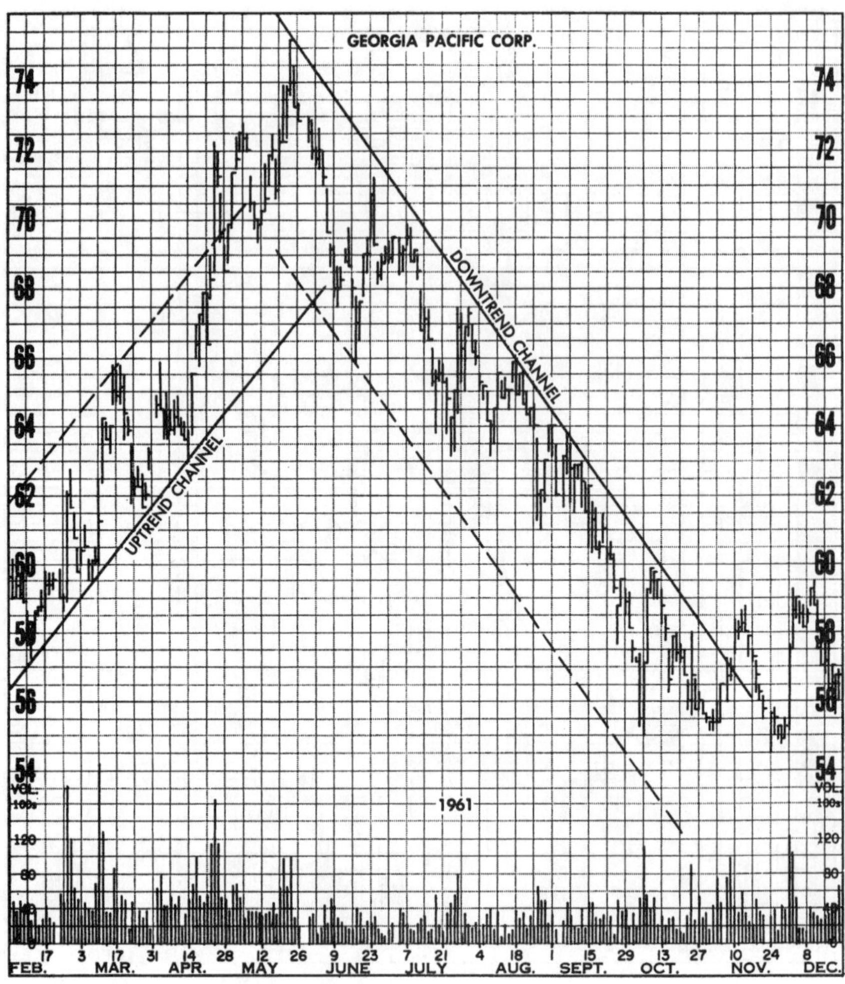

PLATE 2 GEORGIA PACIFIC — Downtrend Line and Channel

Note how prices broke through the upper limit of the uptrend channel at the end of April and, as in the Kerr-McGee chart on the preceding page, this proved to be the start of a "blow-off" which signaled the end of an upswing. Price movements on the downswing stage appeared to be glued to the trendline except for occasional sharp reactions and rallies which served to outline the over-all channel development. This situation proved rather ideal for market tactics based on buying stocks as they hit the lower rims of channels and selling as they approach the upper limits. After the long downtrend line was finally broken by the rally of the first week in November, prices "pulled back" to the trendline at the end of November. Also note how the volume pattern changed in November—increasing on rallies and decreasing on declines.

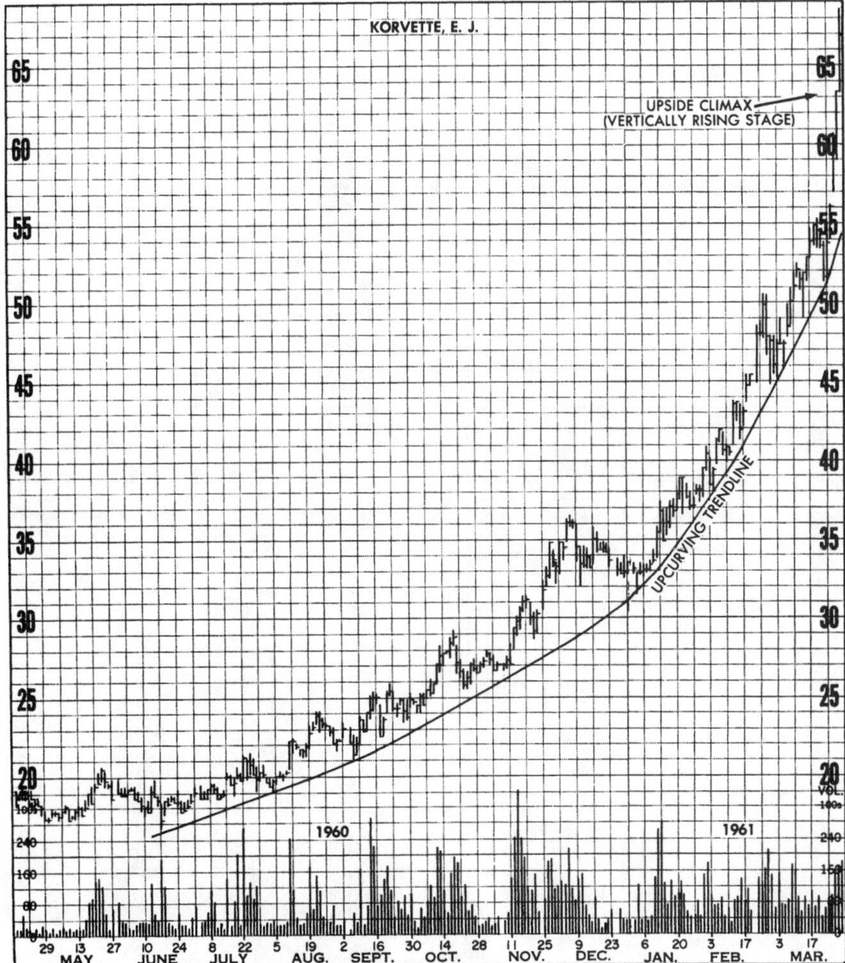

PLATE 3 KORVETTE — Upcurving Trendline

The uptrend which got under way in July and August was preceded by a sideways price movement of several months' duration. The curving was gradual until January, of 1961, when Korvette started to curve sharply higher and by the end of March entered a "blow-off" stage, characterized by a vertical price rise, which marks either a temporary or major turn. As explained in Chapter 2, the curving uptrend line usually leads to this type of market action, but pinpointing the end of the vertically rising stage is extremely difficult, since it can carry a considerable distance in a very short time. In the case above, the high on the last day charted (68½) proved to be a temporary top. Prices reacted all the way back to 47⅜ in June, 1961, before again turning up to an eventual 1961 high of $129.

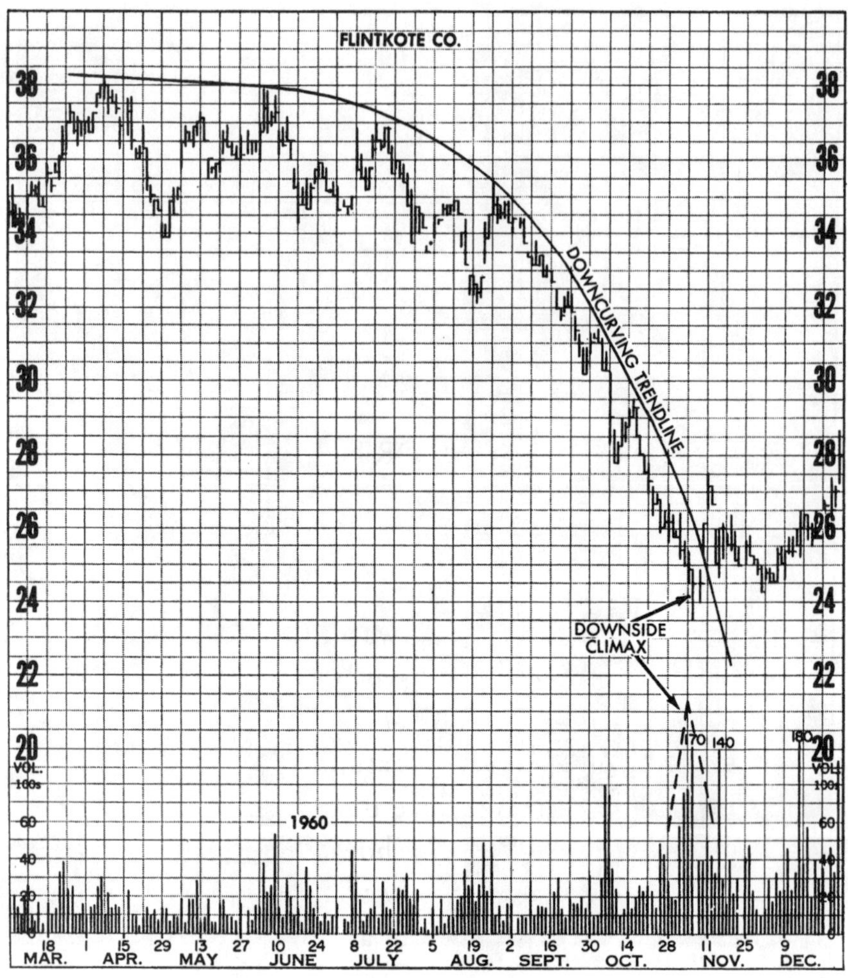

PLATE 4 FLINTKOTE — Downcurving Trendline

The curving downtrend line starts off the same way as the uptrend variety. There is a very gradual curving along the top of the formation and this becomes steeper as the move progresses. As in the chart above, volume remains relatively stable until the decline is well under way and then begins to pick up as the climax stage is reached. The upcurving trendline on the Korvette chart (plate 3) climaxed with very sharp moves but not unusually high volume. In Flintkote, the climax occurred on exceptionally high volume, but day-to-day price moves were not unusual. Climaxes are marked by either wide price moves or exceptional volume or both.

SUPPORT AND RESISTANCE

Have you ever bought a stock, watched it decline in price, and yearned to sell out for what you paid for it? Have you ever sold a stock, watched it go up after you had sold it, and wished you had an opportunity to buy it again at the original price? Well, you are not alone. These are common human reactions, and they show up on the stock charts by creating *support* and *resistance.*

A support level is that price at which one may expect a considerable increase in the demand for a stock, or buying. A resistance level is that price at which one may expect a considerable increase in the supply, or selling. Such levels are not hard to find: for example, any price level where a great deal of stock has changed hands may be pegged as a support or resistance level (the terms are interchangeable, as will be seen). Heavy turnover in a given price area produces what analysts call a congestion range on the chart, as in Figure 11.

FIGURE 11

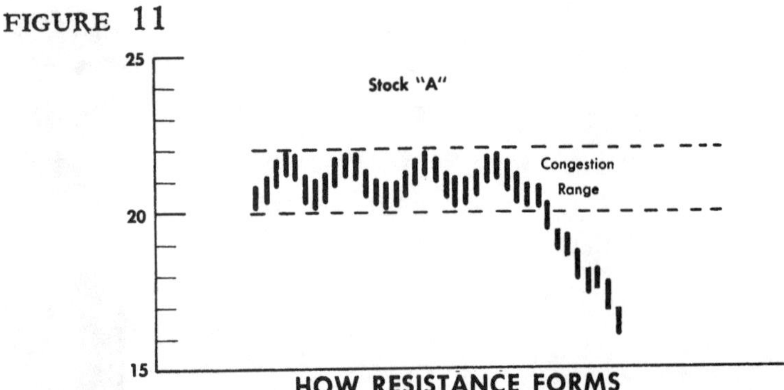

HOW RESISTANCE FORMS

Let's assume that you and hundreds of other investors bought stock A at a range between $20 and $22 a share, and then saw it slip down to $16. The first reaction of the typical buyer will be to hold on, in hope that the stock will rebound, climb above $22, and show a profit that will vindicate the buyer's judgment. However, if stock A remains depressed, many buyers will begin to think it would be great just to break even. So if the stock finally heads back upward, the disposition to sell will grow stronger as it gets closer and closer to the breakeven point. Naturally, the more trading (or congestion) that occurred in the $20-$22 price range, the greater the supply of stock for sale. *Hence, the greater the resistance at that point to a further advance.*

Now, suppose that, after all those investors bought stock A between $20 and $22, it went *up* instead of *down*. The analyst will peg that zone as a *support area*. That is, he would expect that, if stock A, having risen to $25 a share, or more, should slide back, it would meet new buying demand as it returned to the $20-$22 range. There are a number of reasonable explanations. For one thing, those who *sold* out when the stock was at $20-$22 have been kicking themselves all the time it was moving up, and many may be eager to buy back the stock at the price at which they sold it, and thus get "back on board" without embarrassment. They may then say that they were right all along about the great prospects of stock A. Another group—among those who *bought* in the $20-$22 range, or who thought of buying at the time but saw the stock "*get away*" from them—may plan to buy any time it gets back to that price. A third type of major buying may develop from traders who sold short on the rise, and purchase stock to cash in their profits when it falls back.

The analyst usually draws support and resistance points or zones in horizontal lines on his chart. For example, referring to Figure 12, if a stock trades for some time between $20 and $24, the support level becomes outlined at $20 (line A) and the resistance level at $24 (line B). Once prices break above the resistance level of $24, the entire former range (between A and B) becomes a support area, or zone.

FIGURE 12

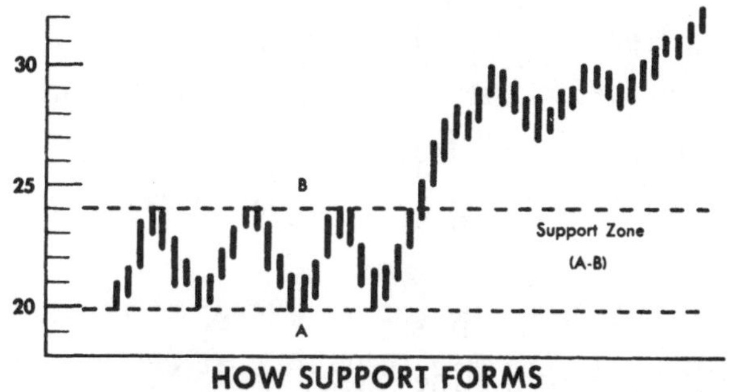

HOW SUPPORT FORMS

As the market develops, a support level may become a resistance level, and vice versa. (See Figure 13.) Suppose that stock B has seesawed between 50 and 55 for several months. During this period, we would correctly label 50 as the support level and 55 as the resistance level. Now, if prices one day break through and close* above 55, this former resistance level automatically becomes a new support level. The many investors who *bought* the stock at 55 at last have found that their judgment was sound, because they now have a paper profit, and some may be willing to buy more at that level. The many who *sold* at 55 may be eager to "get on board again" at that price, for the reason given above.

FIGURE 13

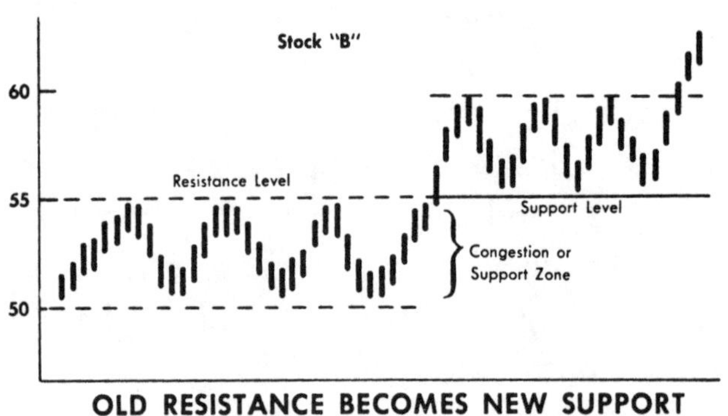

OLD RESISTANCE BECOMES NEW SUPPORT

If the breakout had been *down*—that is, if stock B had fallen below 50, then 50 would switch from a support to a resistance level. All buyers at 50 and over would then have losses and many might want to "break even" if prices get back to 50 or over.

An individual stock (or an average, for that matter) may well meet support or resistance at certain other price

*It might be noted here that analysts regard the closing price as more significant than the "inter-day" high and low, largely on the ground that the average investor looks for, and reacts to, the closing price in his morning newspaper. Stock manipulators have been known to exploit this fact by rigging the last deal of the day, at a price quite different from the bulk of the day's trading.

levels established in the minds of investors, either historically or quite recently. How often does one hear someone say, "I always make money buying such-and-such stock at 20 and selling at 40."* A study of the cyclical stocks (those whose fluctuations follow the ups and downs of the business cycle most closely, such as steels and other basic industrials) reveals that many of them have favorite historic turning points.

Even on the short range, the highs and lows of a stock's fluctuations may have a psychological effect on investors, and thus become minor levels of support and resistance. To illustrate, suppose you held some stock that was rising in the market, and had just about decided to sell, when suddenly it began to drop from new highs. Wouldn't you feel you had missed a golden opportunity to "sell at the top"? And if, while you were brooding about it, your stock rallied to the previous high, wouldn't you be inclined to get out there? If enough buyers feel that way, this high point can form a potent resistance level, even though the first time around, it was reached on very light trading.

THE 50% RULE

When a stock, or the market as a whole, has swung violently up or down, professionals look for a "technical rebound" or "technical reaction." That is, stocks tend to snap back, a third to two-thirds of the way. If stocks have jumped, the quick-trader sells to cash in on profits; if they've dropped, the "bargain hunters" rush in. Then, the stock

*The round number is another common support or resistance level—simply because many investors set their goals in multiples of ten, or even five.

may resume the original trend. In longer-range swings, there is a tendency for support or resistance to develop when the stock retraces half of the ground won, or lost, in the last move. For example, if a stock has advanced from 20 to 60 without serious interruption and then goes into a downtrend, there's a good chance that it will find support at a level midway in the previous advance. Therefore, half of the 40-point gain, or 20 points, can be subtracted from the high to find a potential support level at 40.

FIGURE 14

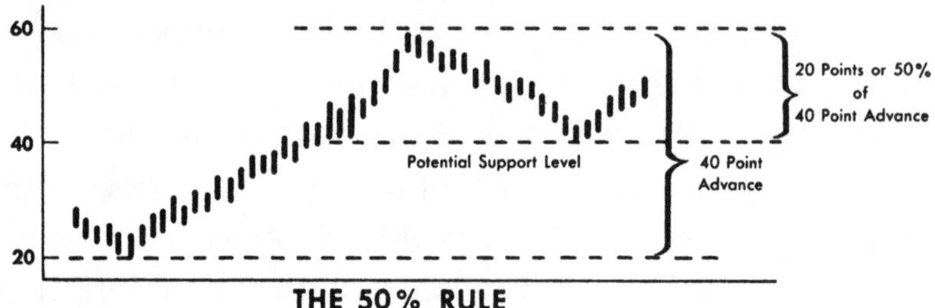

THE 50% RULE

UNUSUAL VOLUME

We have noted that a "congestion range" on the chart shows that a lot of shares have changed hands at a given price for a relatively extended time, and makes this price a probable support or resistance level. Logically, it should not matter too much, however, whether the trading took weeks, or occurred more or less in a relatively short time, as long as trading activity is heavy. A brief flareup of volume during a price movement, *even though it does not appear on the chart to have interrupted the price trend,* often discloses a potent support or resistance area which later proves effective in checking a decline or a rally.

For example, a stock may be rising on average volume and hit, say, $14 a share, whereupon trading suddenly expands sharply. Without any extraordinary acceleration, the price continues to rise, but at about 16, the volume subsides to "normal," or the rate prevailing before the flareup. The price may now continue upward, fall back or move "sideways," but in any case, the chartist will mark this 14-to-16 area as a *High Volume Zone,* and will look for support or resistance in this area. The principle works just as well on a decline, of course. (For examples of High Volume Zones, see the charts at the end of this chapter.)

When the volume of trading expands sharply as a stock reaches an unexpected support or resistance level, the *potency* of that level tends to be increased. Paradoxically, a sharp *drop* in volume sometimes appears to have the same significance! Why this should happen is problematical; perhaps many of those interested in a stock withdraw from the market at what they regard as a significant turning point to see which way it will jump. The drop in volume therefore would be a tip-off to a shift in market psychology associated with a specific price level. In any case, while volume goes *up* more often than *down* at support and resistance levels, it goes down often enough to warrant the consideration of the analyst.

Another note on volume: when a stock breaks out of a congestion zone in which it has been trading, the analyst will, as always, watch the volume to help determine whether the breakout is "valid," rather than just a flash in the pan. It is helpful to know that a valid breakout on the rise (penetrating a resistance level) usually is accompanied by an increase in volume. On the other hand, a valid "downside" breakout (penetrating a support level), usually occurs on light volume at first, which must be confirmed by an increase in volume as the price continues to decline.

SUPPORT AND RESISTANCE IN ACTION

Like trendlines, support and resistance can be found at almost any time and on any chart. In fact, they are the basic components that make up all the more sophisticated patterns that chartists look for in trying to predict price movements. As noted in the preceding chapter, an object in motion (a trend) will continue in motion until it meets an opposing force (support or resistance). The chart reader continually works with both these tools, and he finds that they help each other. Trendlines help confirm support and resistance levels, while support and resistance levels help confirm and anticipate new trendlines.

On daily charts,* it is prudent to consider the *bottom* of a support zone as more valid than the *top*. Very frequently, a rising stock will react back *into* a support zone and then resume its advance. (See Figure 15.) A new support level may then form *within* the previous support zone, and become the next valid support. Illustrations of support and resistance analysis appear at the end of the chapter.

FIGURE 15

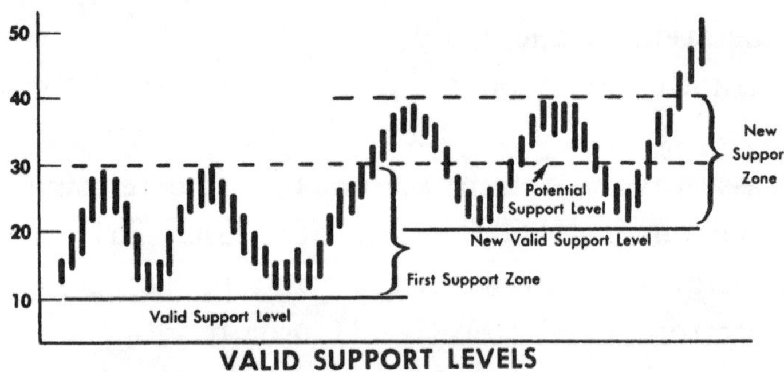

VALID SUPPORT LEVELS

*Weekly and monthly charts also reveal support and resistance levels, and are convenient for spotting long-established, or "historic" levels of individual stocks, as mentioned earlier. The potency of resistance and support levels has a tendency to fade with time, but the chartist will find many surprising examples which have proved to be significant even after several years have elapsed.

The study of support and resistance can tell the investor whether his ship is on course. As long as support levels hold firm, he can feel that his stock is doing well, and he may buy more. If his stock breaks through a support level, he has cause for concern, and may consider selling out.

Some traders use their studies of support and resistance to set up practical trading systems. They *buy* when stocks have fallen to support levels, or when stocks have risen and broken through resistance levels. They sell when stocks hit resistance levels or fall through support levels.

Another technique may be as follows: If a stock breaks out of a trading range of 50-55 and climbs, say, to 58, the previous resistance point of 55 becomes a support zone. The short-swing trader may not wish to hold on to the stock if, on a downswing, it penetrates the 55 level. Longer-range traders may be content to hold the stock as long as the lower level of the support zone (50) is not broken.

The sophisticated investor uses the support-and-resistance concept to help him decide in advance at what price he should instruct his broker to sell, in order to cash in his profits on a market rise. In a major downtrend, he uses it to find a level where a rally is likely to develop, at which point he may close out a short position (buy stock cheaply to replace shares he sold short at a higher price), or he may plan new investment buying.

Now, having sharpened our basic tools of trendlines and support-and-resistance, we are ready to proceed to the most fascinating aspect of chart reading—the remarkable formations that signal major turning points in the market.

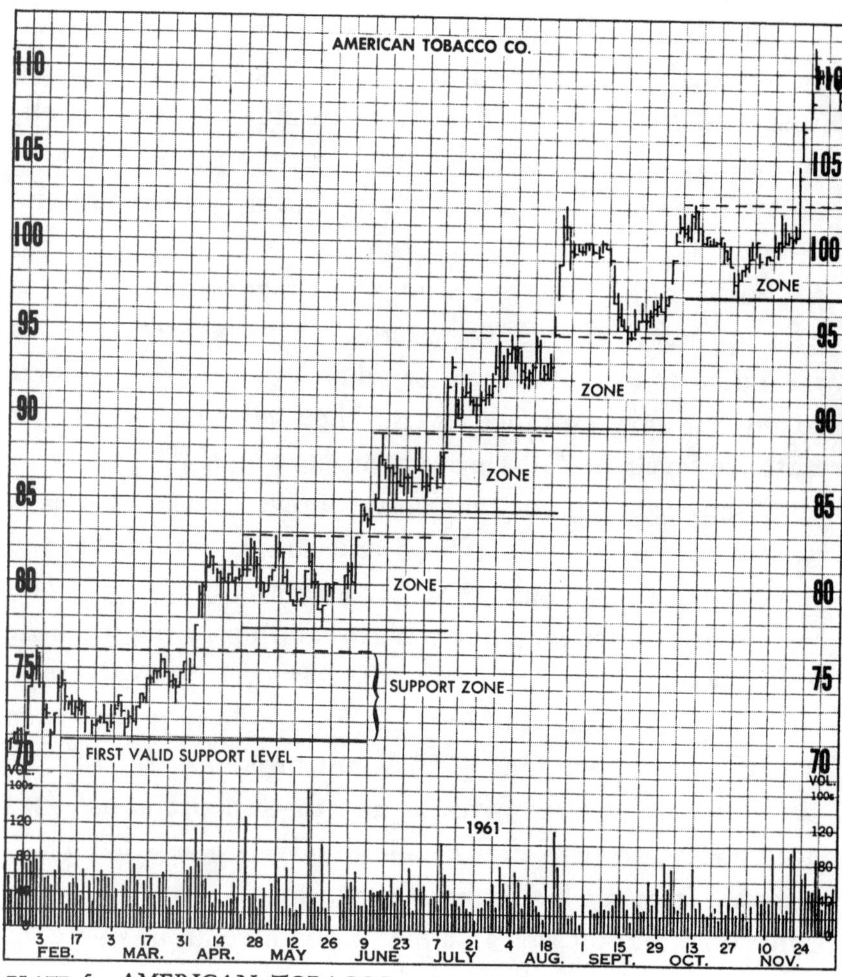

PLATE 5 AMERICAN TOBACCO — Support Levels

The advance depicted above is really the continuation of a long-range uptrend begun in 1958. It shows a nearly ideal example of support zones in action. Practically no part of the support zone formed after each thrust into new high ground was violated. This is not a rare occurrence, but day-to-day analysis of support zones in action will indicate that support zones are as likely to be subject to some penetration than not. The significant part of the formation is the "valid support line" (solid horizontal lines). As long as this line marking the lower part of the support zone holds, your investment ship can be considered to be "on course". Caution: Always draw your "valid support line" after prices have emerged out of a new congestion area on the upside.

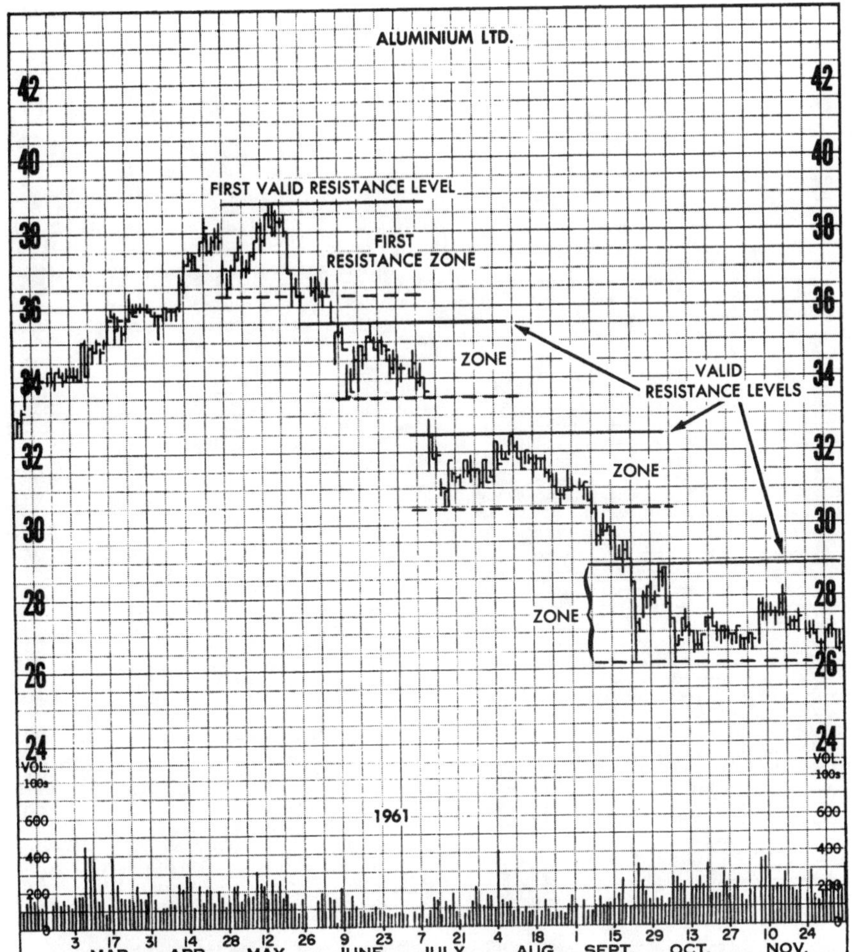

PLATE 6 ALUMINIUM LTD. — Resistance Levels

The resistance lines here are similar to the support lines in the preceding chart. Each time a new low was made from June on, it proved impenetrable to subsequent rallies. The resistance zone is less likely to be violated in a downtrend than the support zone in an uptrend—nevertheless, the "valid resistance level" is still the more significant chart point to watch in following a decline. Note: An interesting "wedge" top is outlined here. This formation is not covered until you get to chapter 10, so disregard it for the time being. Refer back to this illustration at the end of that chapter.

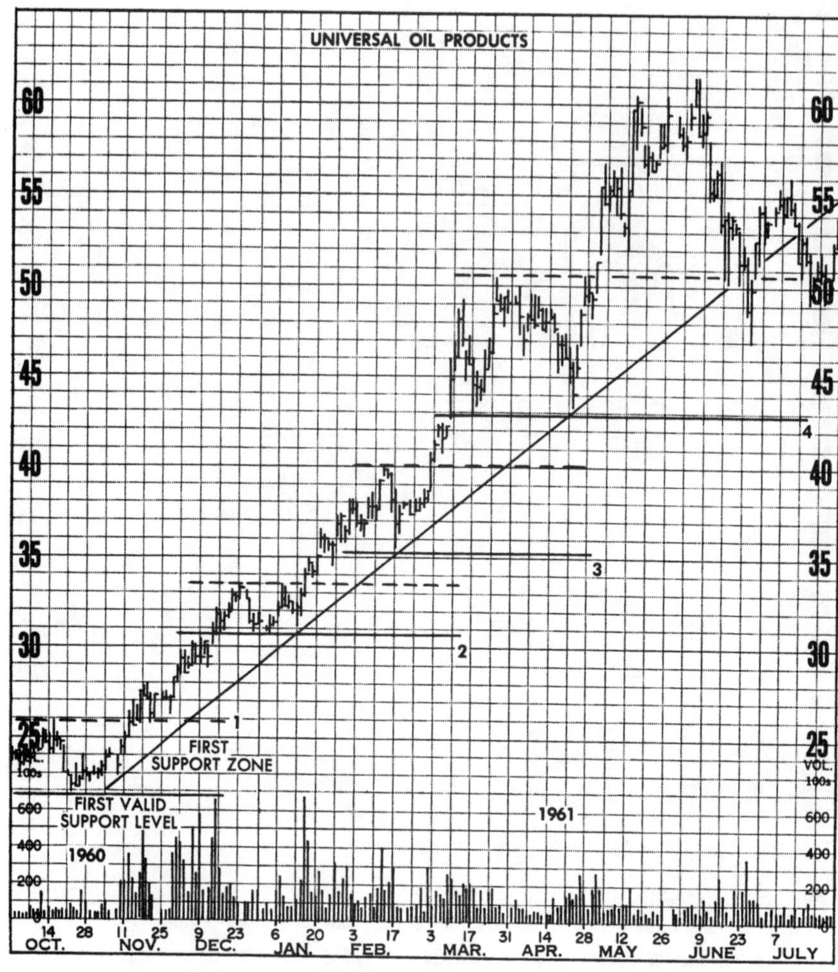

PLATE 7 UNIVERSAL OIL PRODUCTS—
Valid Support Levels and Support Zones

Prices of UOP almost tripled in less than eight months without violating a trendline or even threatening a previous support zone. The technique used to draw in the support zones was rather simple and did not depend on hindsight. Each time that prices moved to new highs out of a congestion area, the valid support line (solid line) could be drawn along the lows, and the upper line of the support zone (dotted line) drawn along the highs of the same congestion area. Support zones are outlined and valid support lines are numbered 1 to 4 to mark the advance. All support zones held until June, when prices declined into the fourth or latest support zone (and broke the trendline). This could have been interpreted as a warning; however, the valid support level (4), became the critical chartline to watch, rather than the major trendline. Actually, this support level held and, by the end of 1961, prices reached 69.

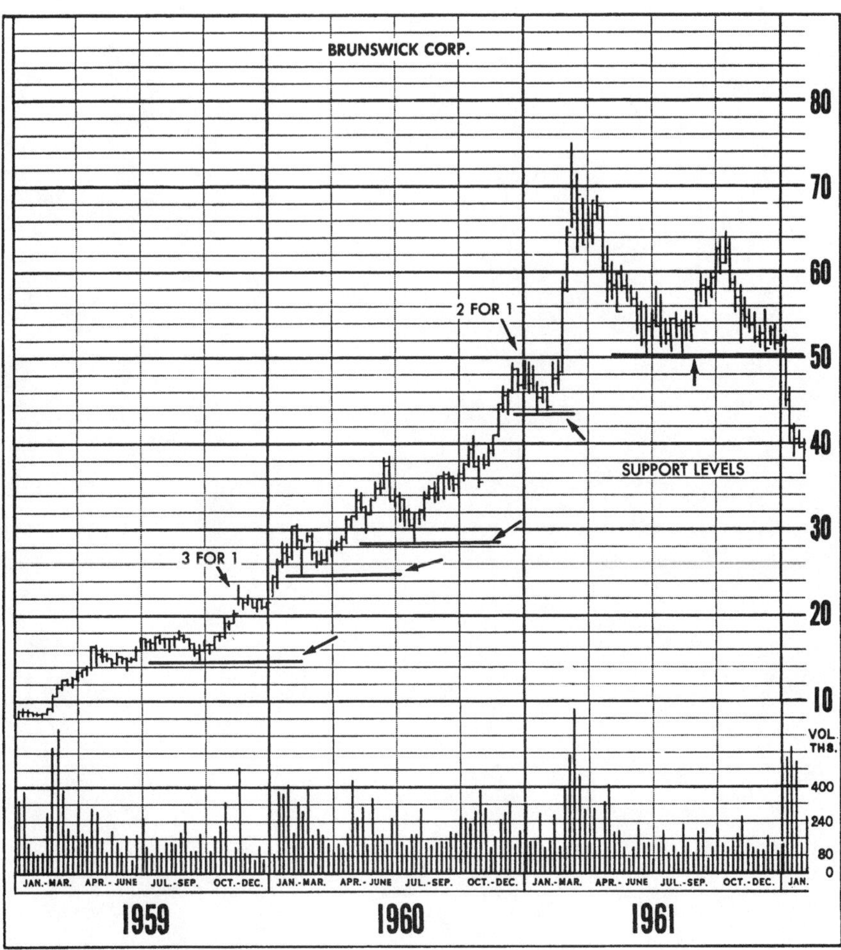

PLATE 8 BRUNSWICK (Weekly Range Chart) — Support and Resistance

All of the chart considerations in the price analysis of a daily chart also will appear on longer range charts such as weekly high, low and close charts, and monthly range charts. The first of several illustrations in this book using weekly range charts is the weekly high, low and close chart of Brunswick Corp. Prices (adjusted) rose from 9 in 1959 to 74⅞ in 1961. Valid support levels were not violated, and the trend was not seriously challenged until the second quarter of 1961. The first sign of important weakness occurred when the upcurving trendline was broken. This stamped the vertical price rise on tremendous volume in February and March as a possible climax of the long bull move. In mid-1961, a congestion range formed (50-58) and prices rallied for a test of the all-time high, but fell short. The support line at 50 helped to hold prices for 9 weeks, but prices broke through on volume and plunged downward.

HEAD AND SHOULDERS

Of all the chart patterns that signal a reversal of trend, the "Head and Shoulders" is by far the best known. It often stands out sharply, and it's almost always possible to find one of them in the process of unfolding on some chart in one's collection. Experienced chartists are fond of it as among the most reliable of indicators, while newcomers to chart analysis seize upon it as an early opportunity to put their theories to a practical test in the market.

As in abstract art, one should not expect the picture of a Head and Shoulders closely to resemble the real thing. Over-simplified, a Head and Shoulders (right-side up, as in Figure 16) simply portrays three successive rallies and reactions, with the second one reaching a higher point than either of the others. The failure of the third rally to equal the peak of the second is a warning that a major uptrend may have come to an end. Conversely, a *bottom* Head and Shoulders, found upside down following a declining trend, suggests that an upturn lies ahead. Let's examine the three phases of the Head and Shoulders top in detail:

FIGURE 16

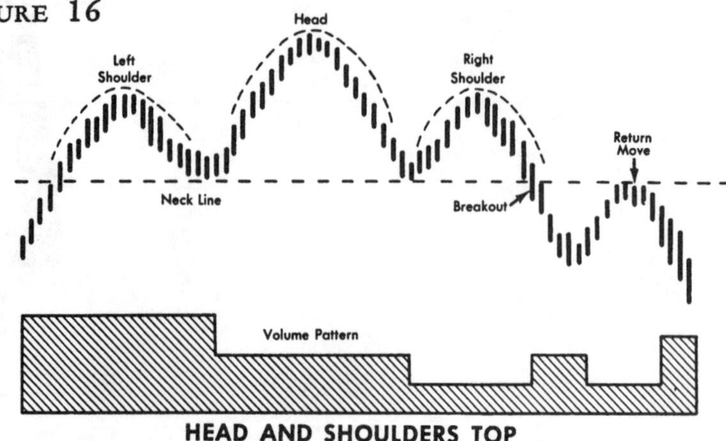

HEAD AND SHOULDERS TOP

1. *Left Shoulder*—This forms when an upturn of some duration reaches a climax in a rally, which is followed by a reaction. Volume is important. It should expand materially on the rally, and contract noticeably on the reaction. Overall volume is heavy during the formation of the left shoulder.

2. *The Head*—A second rally carries the stock higher than the first one, but is followed by a reaction that erases just about all the gain, leaving the price in the vicinity of the previous low. Volume is high on the rally phase, but overall volume usually is not quite so high as during the left shoulder.

3. *Right Shoulder*—A third rally *fails to reach the height of the Head before another reaction sets in.* The formation of a right shoulder is a decided manifestation of weakness. Yet it is in this area that most chart misreadings are apt to occur. These can be avoided if particular attention is directed to volume during the building of the right shoulder. If volume *contracts* noticeably on this rally, one may

take it as strong evidence that the price structure has been weakened. If, however, the volume *increases,* beware of a false signal, no matter how ideally the picture may have been unfolding.

No Head and Shoulders should be regarded as complete until the price breaks down below a line drawn tangent with the lows of the left and right shoulders. This is called the Neckline. (Some advanced students believe it makes some difference of degree whether the Neckline slants up or down, or is horizontal, but this is debatable, and in any case need not concern us here.)

Once the Head and Shoulders is completed, more often than not a rally will carry the price back to the Neckline. This is called the *Return Move.* Whether a stock will make such a move often depends on conditions in the general market. If the market as a whole is turning strongly upward, a return move in the stock is quite likely. On the other hand, if the general tone is soft, there may be no return move. The same applies to trends of the industry that includes this stock: if it's an oil, and the oils are rallying, we may look for a return move, etc. Since outside factors must be considered, it's not feasible to set down a hard and fast rule.

THE HEAD AND SHOULDERS BOTTOM

As indicated, the inverse Head and Shoulders (or Head and Shoulders bottom), looks exactly the same on the chart as a Head-and-Shoulders top, except that it's upside down, and marks the end of a downtrend rather than the end of an advance. But the volume develops somewhat differently, and since volume plays a major role in determining whether any pattern is valid, it is worthwhile to review the components of an inverse Head and Shoulders:

FIGURE 17

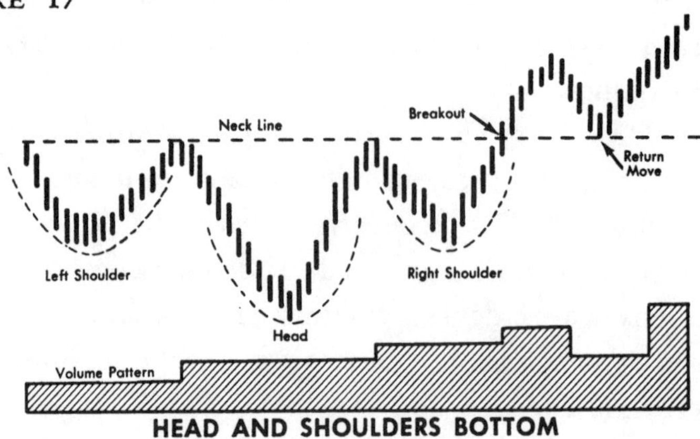

HEAD AND SHOULDERS BOTTOM

1. *The Left Shoulder*—A downtrend, under way for some time, reaches a climax in a sharp slide, which is followed by a rally. Volume expands materially on the decline, and contracts noticeably on the rally.

2. *The Head*—A second decline carries the stock below the low point of the left shoulder; then a second rally carries it back to the vicinity of the previous rally's high. Volume increases on the second decline, as compared with the rally that preceded it, but it usually does not equal the volume of the first decline. Volume should increase again on the second rally and overall volume during the formation of the head is slightly greater than during the building of the left shoulder.

3. *The Right Shoulder*—A third decline fails to reach the low of the second, and another rally develops. Volume should taper off decidedly on this decline, and pick up sharply on the rally, *remaining high right through the breaking of the neckline*. This is an extremely important test of any Head and Shoulders bottom. If the volume is

not there, one would be especially wary of the possibility of a false move, no matter how ideally the chart picture may have unfolded. If the volume *is* there, the break through the neckline completes and confirms the pattern.

Again, no hard and fast rule can be set down regarding the probability of a return move. The trend of the general market or of the specific group of stocks may have some bearing on the situation. It has been suggested that a return move is more likely to follow a bottom pattern than a top one, but no statistical proof of this is at hand.

HOW IT HAPPENS

Like any other chart pattern, the Head and Shoulders describes what occurs when buyers meet sellers under certain circumstances. Let us try to depict, in the form of a diagram, just how different groups of investors react psychologically—and with their money—during the different phases of a Head and Shoulders, which we might call a drama in three acts. Our cast of characters is as follows:

GROUP A — Persons who bought stock before or during an uptrend, and are now ready to sell and take their profits.

GROUP B — Persons who missed the uptrend, but are now ready to buy the stock at "bargain" prices during a technical reaction.

GROUP C — Persons who, like Group B, have missed the uptrend and want to buy on the reaction, but wait too long and "reach" for the market on its rally to new highs.

GROUP D — Persons who have missed the uptrend and the first reaction, but seize on the second reaction as a "last chance" to get that bargain price.

GROUP E Same characters as in Group C, except that they are now would-be sellers. Having seen their new purchases turn into paper losses, they have now decided, "If the price gets back up to where I can break even, or take just a small loss, I'll sell."

GROUP F Remnants of Group A, plus a smattering of trades in each of the other groups, who now all show losses on their purchases.

Here is how the drama develops, in diagram form:

FIGURE 18

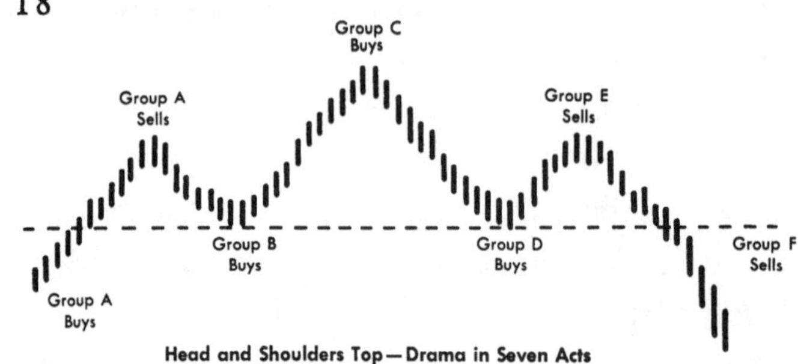

Head and Shoulders Top—Drama in Seven Acts

MORE PICASSO THAN RENOIR

Let us emphasize here what we suggested at the beginning—that the term "Head and Shoulders" is a pretty abstract and highly imaginary title for a pattern of market behavior. As with all other patterns of behavior involving people and many other unpredictable elements, chart configurations do not follow a rigid formula. Sometimes the Head is not a point, or a curve, but a flat-top, representing a "sideways congestion range." Sometimes the shoulders are deformed: one does not appear to balance the other. And sometimes, Complex Head and Shoulders take form, which is to say that a small pattern is contained within a larger one, or that there are two left shoulders, two heads and two right shoulders. This need not frighten a public that pays fortunes for paintings by Picasso. (For the chart variety, see Figure 19.)

In spite of such variations, the alert chart reader should be able to detect in many actual market charts behavior that is basically similar to that of the classic Head and Shoulders we described earlier. If this similarity is there, it will serve as an indicator of a probable reversal in trend.

FIGURE 19

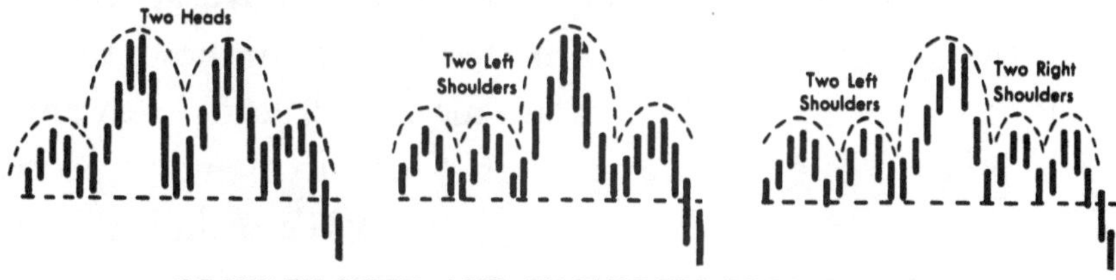

COMPLEX HEAD AND SHOULDERS FORMATIONS

OBJECTIVES

Having found a reversal pattern such as a Head and Shoulders, which indicates that a stock that has been rising is now likely to fall, or vice versa, we meet another important question: *How far will it go?*

We know enough now to get aboard the train (i.e.—buy stock for the rise, or sell short for the decline), but where do we get off? To "project the move" or "compute the objectives" calls for a diligent assessment of a number of factors. We'll discuss these factors here in closer detail than we have seen in previous studies of the subject. It's worth it. We can't hit the objective of a price swing right on the nose every time, but we can with practice achieve a high batting average.

FIGURE 20

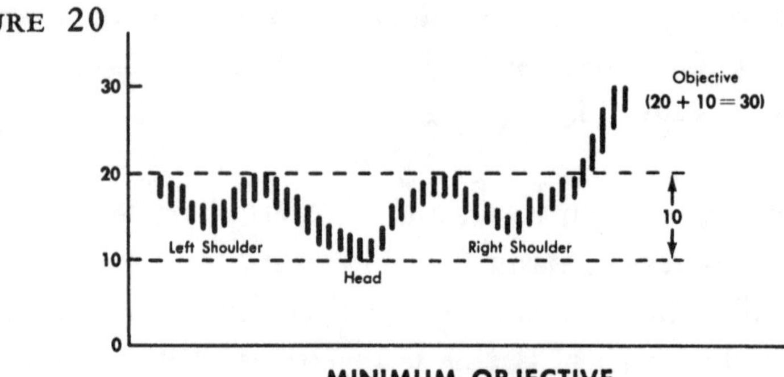

MINIMUM OBJECTIVE

Now, a common rule of thumb applied to Head and Shoulders formations is that, once the pattern has been completed, the stock in its reversal swing will move at least as far again as the distance from the top of the head to the neckline. (See Figure 20.) This rule is well known to analysts, but it does not go far enough. Our selection of a probable objective must take into account other technical factors, such as, in the order of importance:

1. What is the general market doing?
2. How does the current price stand in relation to the historic price scale of our stock?
3. Where are major levels of support or resistance to be met?

FIGURE 21

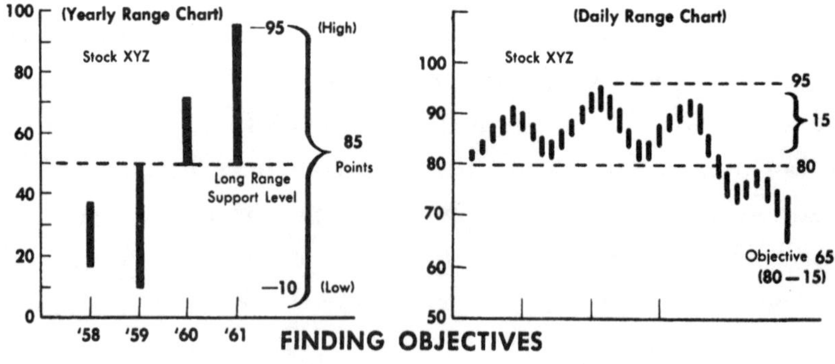

FINDING OBJECTIVES

For a practice run, let's assume that Stock XYZ has completed a well defined Head and Shoulders top. (Figure 21.) Should we sell? And if so, when do we buy back? If the setback is going to be minor and we like our stock for the long haul, it's hardly worth selling. If the move is intermediate, we'd consider selling, but still might decide not to, because of the capital-gains tax we'd have to pay on our profits. On the other hand, if a major slump is impending, we want out. Well, let's see. Like an airline pilot who runs down a checklist to determine whether it's safe to take off, let's run down our checklist (Questions (1.), (2.) and (3.) above) to see whether it's prudent to hold or sell:

1. The market as a whole offers no decisive clue. Stocks have been moving irregularly "sideways" with considerable selectivity by the public, and our own industry group has been mixed.
2. XYZ hit an all-time high of 95 at the top of the Head, formed a Right Shoulder, broke through the neckline at 80 and then effected a return move to 80, where it now stands. Three years ago it hit an all-time low of 10. That means that, at the top, it had risen 850% in three years. Obviously then, the stock is historically high, and there is ample room to decline—or is there?
3. A long range chart reveals that the last major area of "congestion" or "consolidation" with considerable trading occurred at 50. *There is no other important support visible at a higher price*. Thus, again, there is another potential support area which we discussed in a previous chapter, when we noted that stocks often tend to retrace 50%

of a major move, and then meet support or resistance. This is easily computed. Over a period of three years, XYZ rose from 10 to 95, or 85 points. Half of 85 is 42½. Subtract that from 95, and you get 52½. Since that is relatively close to 50, where strong support is indicated, we had better rely on the latter figure.

But we have not yet considered our rule of thumb for the swing following a Head and Shoulders formation. In this case, the distance from Head (95) to the Neckline (80) is 15 points, so that we may expect XYZ to drop to 65. And there's a good chance that it will go to 52½ or 50. On the basis of these findings, XYZ is an excellent candidate to be sold for a minimum decline of 15 points.

THE HEAD AND SHOULDERS FAILURE PATTERN

So far, we have discussed patterns that have been completed. The stocks have broken through the Necklines, and we know which way they are probably going. But sometimes a Head and Shoulders formation, or one of its variations, will develop in a perfectly normal fashion, but will fail to penetrate the neckline. (See Figure 22.) Instead, the stock moves "sideways," fluctuating indecisively. We know, then, that a reversal pattern has *not* developed. But we also know that the price activity within this area may be preparing a significant trend move in either direction.

This activity is much like that of a car stuck in snow or mud. By a judicious shifting of gears, the motorist causes the vehicle to rock back and forth. When the momentum is just right, he steps on the gas and away he goes, forward or in reverse—at least, so he hopes. In a Head and Shoulders

Failure Pattern, the up-and-down movement within a sideways range establishes a momentum, and at just the right moment—a penetration of the top or bottom line of the trading range—prices gain traction, and a new trend is established. This type of formation can support a major move.

FIGURE 22

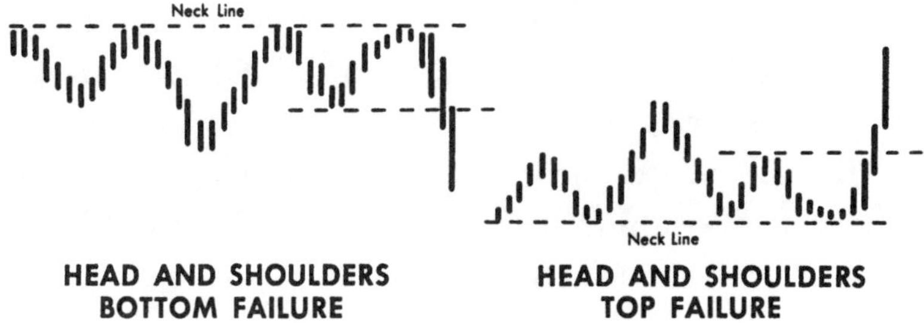

TACTICS

It's time now to put our theory to work. For review, we present at the end of the chapter actual case histories of six stocks. These charts were selected to illustrate interesting chart formations and problems in computing objectives. No doubt other stock charts would have served as well, if not better, but given basically similar patterns, the principles and results would have been the same.

Our Head-and-Shoulders theory, and a study of these case histories, demonstrate an obvious conclusion: *The investor should make his commitment, as a general rule, when a stock breaks through the Neckline.*

However, an alert and experienced investor may act as early as during the formation of the Right Shoulder, *if there is strong reason to believe that the formation will be completed*. Such reason will exist if—

1. The relationship of the current price to the historic price scale is favorable to a reversal of the previous extended trend.
2. The previous trend has run into strong support or resistance.
3. Volume indications have been measuring up to standards for a Head and Shoulders formation.
4. The general market is neutral or headed in the direction opposite the one that our stock had been following before the Head and Shoulders began to form.

In such a case, the investor may take action very close to the top or bottom of a major swing, which would be calling his shots very neatly, indeed.

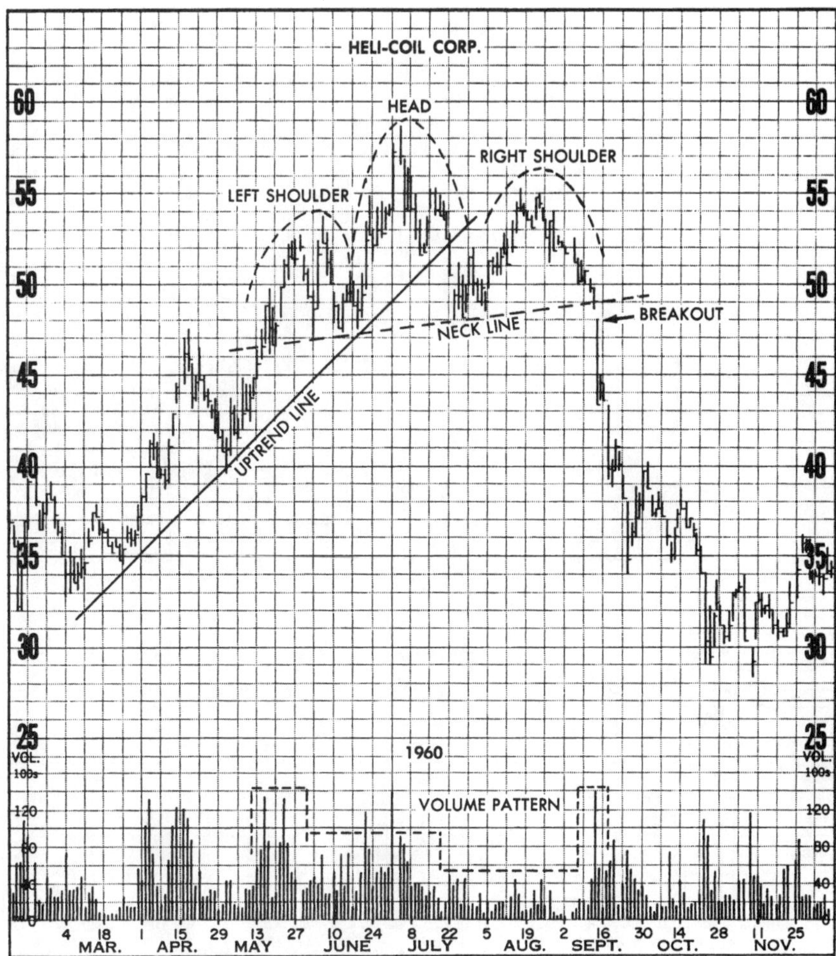

PLATE 9 HELI-COIL — Head & Shoulders Top

This large and well-defined Head & Shoulders top can be easily identified without the superimposed outline and labels. For the chartist following prices in June, the change in volume pattern might have alerted him to a possible change in trend. The rally to new highs was accompanied by somewhat reduced volume, compared with the previous rally in May. Then the breaking of the trendline on July 22 lent confirmation that the advance was in danger of reversing. The third important clue was the building of the right shoulder on very low volume. And finally, the breaking of the neckline, which in this case was also a valid support line, left little doubt that selling pressure, or the supply of stock, was then greater than buying pressure, or the demand. In this case, the third clue—the right shoulder on unusually low volume—should have been sufficient chart evidence for one to anticipate the pattern and take profits not far from the top of the move.

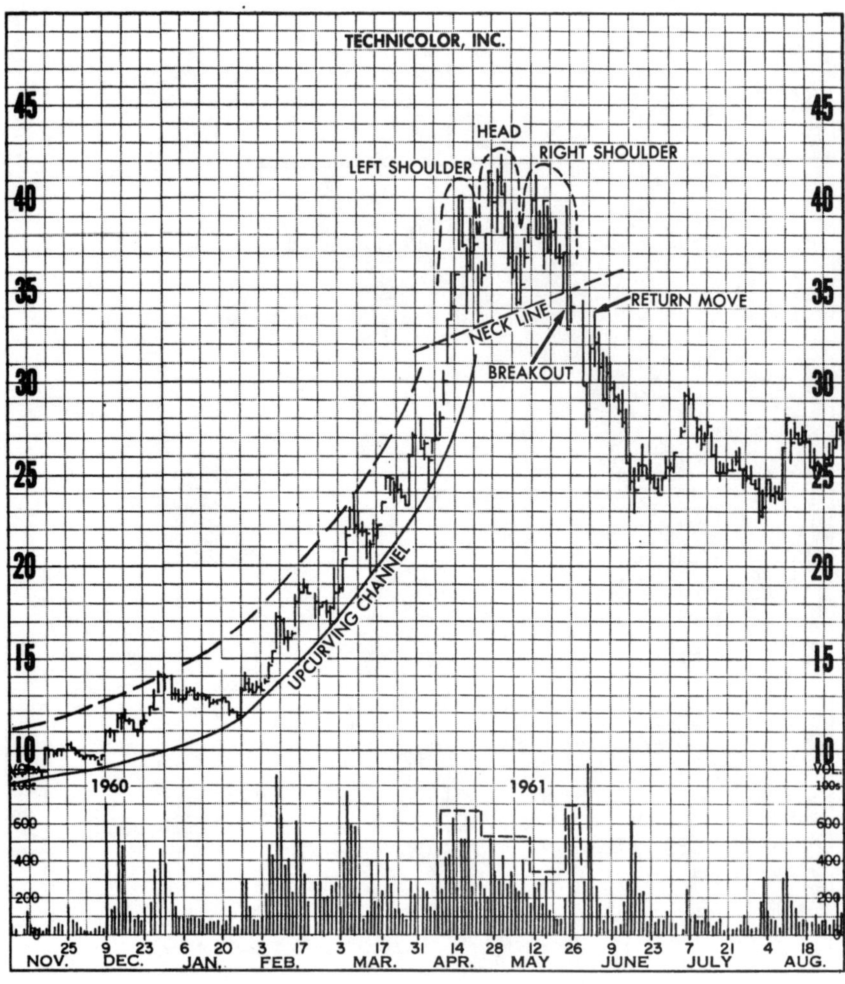

PLATE 10 TECHNICOLOR — Head & Shoulders Top

In price and volume behavior, this April-May top was almost an ideal Head & Shoulders formation, yet the closeness of the shoulders to the head (1 to 2 points) could argue strongly for those who see Triple Tops. As can be seen from the chart, prices formed a well-defined upcurving trendline and channel, reaching a climax with vertically rising prices on high volume. High volume also marked the left shoulder. Activity was progressively lower for the head and right shoulder. The breaking of the neckline was on high volume, and the return on lower volume. Although not shown, prices rallied in October for a test of the top pattern (now a resistance area) and were thrown back from about the 36 level, eventually declining to around 21.

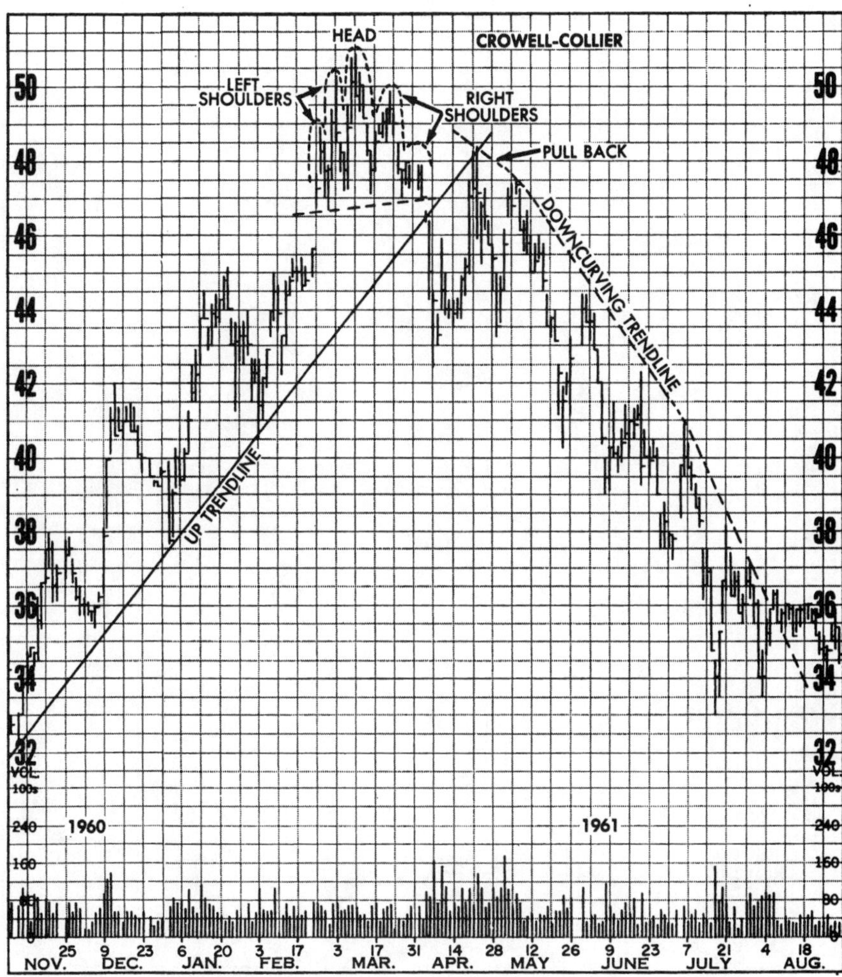

PLATE 11 CROWELL-COLLIER — Complex Head & Shoulders Top

If all formations were this clear, chart reading would be a snap. From November through March, prices followed an uptrend line as if they were glued to it. Then a small Head & Shoulders top formed and prices broke the neckline and the long uptrend line simultaneously. This reversed the trend, and prices then closely traced out a downcurving trendline. The Head & Shoulders top here has two left and two right shoulders, which are interesting for their symmetry. But the characteristic Head & Shoulders volume pattern is missing, which would support those analysts who prefer to call this formation a Triple Top. Also, note how the "return move" did not stop at the neckline, but did halt exactly at the previous major uptrend line, illustrating the magnetic pullback effect common to most trendline breaks. Whether one called it a Head & Shoulders or a Triple Top, the forecasting implications were the same.

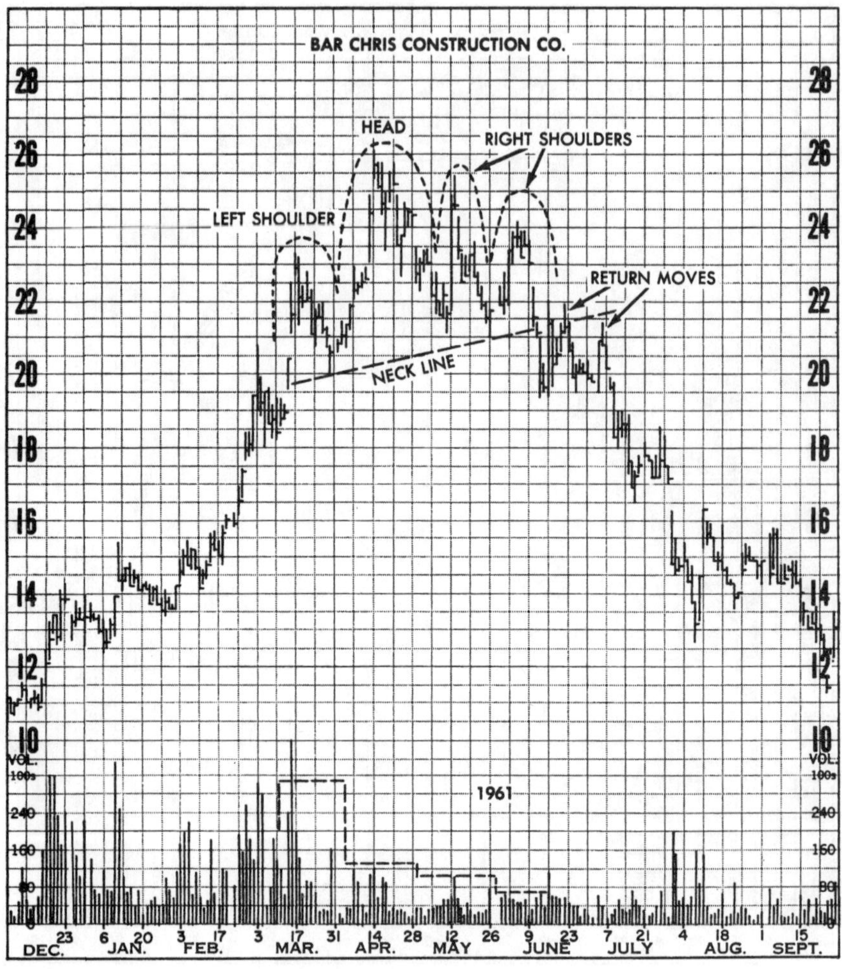

PLATE 12 BAR CHRIS CONSTRUCTION CO.—
Complex Head & Shoulders Top

This is another chart where an upcurving trendline climaxed and led to a Head & Shoulders top. This one has only one left shoulder, but two right shoulders. Coincidentally, after the neckline was broken in June, there were two return moves, apparently balancing the two right shoulders. This should not be taken as typical. As a matter of fact, more often than not, Head & Shoulder tops don't have a return move, even the complex varieties. This top proved to be quite potent. By February, 1962, prices dropped to $9, completely wiping out the 1961 advance. After the reader has finished this book, a review of this chart will disclose Flags, Pennants, Triangles, Measuring Gaps and Exhaust Gaps.

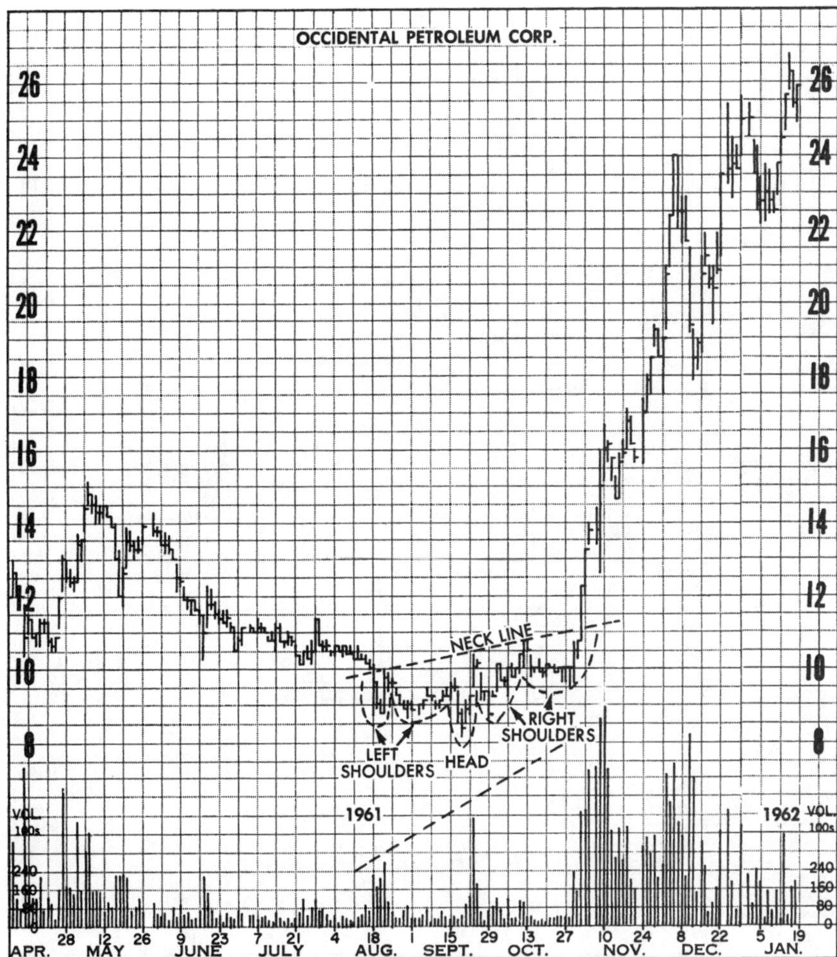

PLATE 13 OCCIDENTAL PETROLEUM— Complex Head & Shoulders Bottom

This Head & Shoulders bottom has two left shoulders, one head and two right shoulders, and it is upslanting. The breakthrough of the neckline came on tremendous volume and there was no return move to the neckline after the breakout. The price rose to 24 virtually without interruption, on feverish volume. The stock price just about tripled in twelve weeks. Any slowdown of an advance accompanied by such high volume would be considered an adverse development, since it would mean that the supply of stock was sufficient to meet the most urgent demand. The more advanced chartist will also note the formation of a small Diamond within the overall complex Head & Shoulders bottom. In this case, the Diamond was overshadowed by the longer formation and has little chart significance. Other patterns often form within Heads & Shoulders, especially Triangles.

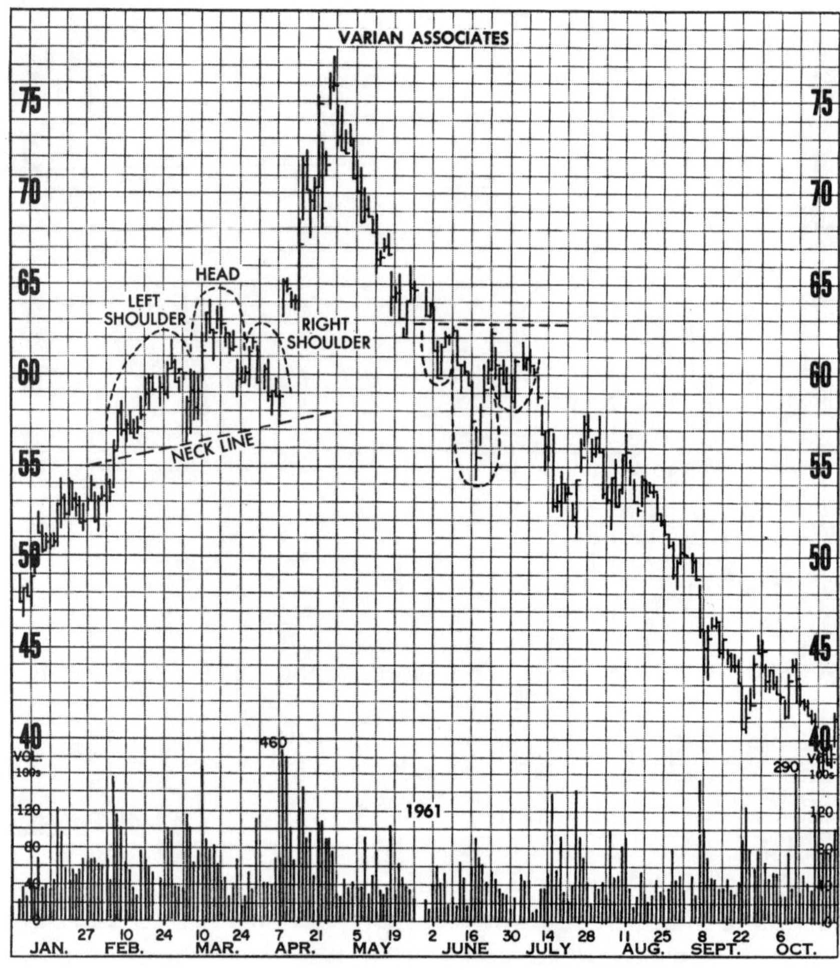

PLATE 14 VARIAN ASSOCIATES — Head & Shoulders Failure Patterns

This illustration contains two interesting examples of Head & Shoulders failure patterns. A Head & Shoulders top appeared to be forming between February and April. Just as prices were easing for a test of the "neckline", prices opened on April 8, 4 points higher than the previous day's close, on tremendous volume. Prices jumped above the right shoulder and head, thus signaling a strong advance. Again (in June,) and around the same level, prices attempted to outline a Head & Shoulders bottom. But before the neckline could be broken, prices reacted sharply to new lows, thus tipping off a resumption of the decline. (After completing chapter 7, you will be able to identify the top as a true V formation.)

DOUBLE TOPS AND BOTTOMS

Among the most familiar of chart patterns—and yet among the most deceptive—are the Double Tops and Bottoms. Experienced analysts have long recognized them as common patterns of market behavior at a turning point, or reversal, and therefore as highly valuable. Beginners love them, because they tend to see Double Tops and Bottoms everywhere.

The *Double Top* (Figure 23) resembles the letter *M* and is often called an *M* formation. Prices rise sharply to a pivot *A,* fall back part way to *B,* rally to about the level of *A* at point *C,* and then decline past the previous reaction low set by *B*. Similarly, as might be expected, the *Double Bottom* is often called a *W* formation.

FIGURE 23

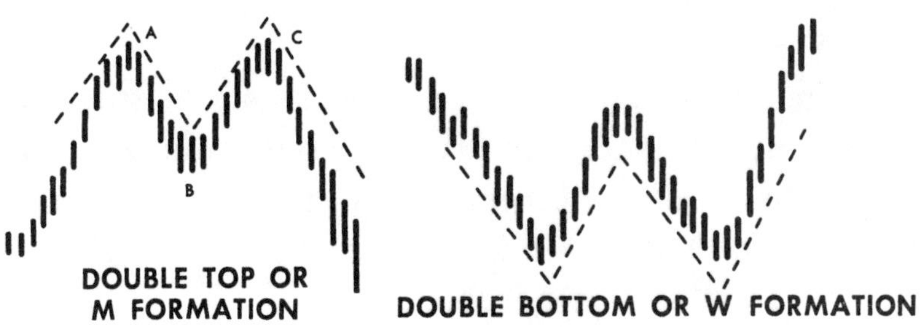

Because the normal movement of stocks on a daily chart takes the form of a zigzag line, the beginning analyst may tend to read a Double Top or Bottom into every movement. In actual practice, *very few formations that start out looking like Double Tops or Bottoms end up as true patterns*. Furthermore, the true ones are not easily diagnosed *until the reversals in trend have become pronounced and prices already have moved substantially*.

One of the main reasons for the trouble here is that, as we pointed out in a previous chapter, a stock *normally* meets resistance at a previous high, and support at a previous low. This often causes it to hesitate, or pull back a bit. But, it may be only a brief pause before the stock absorbs all the supply or demand waiting at this point, and then easily penetrates the level and resumes its advance. To the beginner, any hesitation may look like the top of an *M* or bottom of a *W*. More often than not, it is only routine price action within any one of a host of other chart configurations.

Let's examine a true Double Top in terms of market psychology. The first peak represents the price level where a big enough supply of stock was put on the market to satisfy all demands and cause a moderate reaction. This reaction may reflect selling based on a combination of motives, such as a fairly widespread decision to cash in on profits, and a well-informed view that, for various reasons, the stock has gone about as high as it's likely to go for the time being.

After the reaction, "weak" holders of the stock may feel they missed an opportunity to sell out at the top. When "bargain hunters" and other optimists move in, running the price back to its previous peak, these sellers who missed the first peak rush to unload. In addition, some of those who sold the first time have more stock to offer at the same price. The supply therefore again increases enough to drive the stock down. Now, if prices drop down through the previous reaction low, it is clear that the demand for stock at prices in the top area has been satisfied, and that the supply of stock is still heavier than the demand. *With an advance thus ruled out, the path of least resistance leads downward.*

VOLUME

The *normal* volume pattern of a Double Top is a marked increase in trading around each of the peaks. However—and here's a big however—a study of valid Double Tops and Bottoms reveals a considerable variation in volume behavior. Trading may be light on one peak, and heavy on the other. In fact, some very potent tops and bottoms have formed on unusually light volume throughout. The best rule appears to be this: *Heavy volume around one or both peaks, or any unusual change in volume, such as a notable drop in activity, tends to confirm the development of a Double Top or Bottom.*

VARIATIONS

Many Double Tops that form on daily charts show one peak slightly higher than the other, but still mark a true reversal pattern (Figure 24). Sometimes, a stock that's completing a Double Top or Bottom may hesitate, and build a small *platform,* or congestion range, before the main move gets underway. This more often occurs in a Double Bottom. The platform takes shape in the area just beyond the middle leg of the W, or just at the breakout area.

FIGURE 24

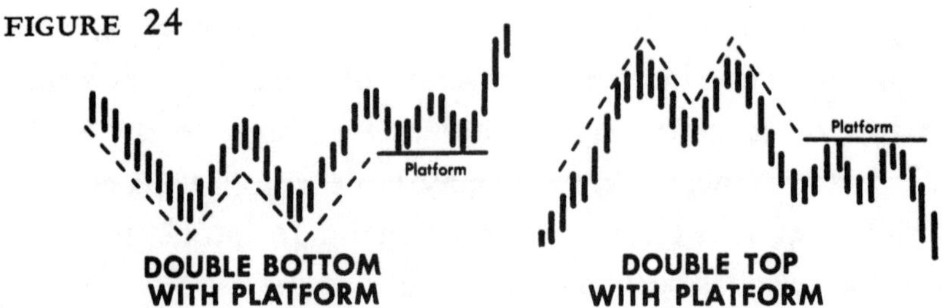

The *Triple* Top or bottom is a well-known, and valid, variation (Fig. 25) on daily hi-low charts, although somewhat rare on weekly or monthly range charts. In this case, the stock declines from the second peak of what is shaping up as a Double Top, but runs into support buying around the level of the previous low. Instead of breaking through and completing the Double Top, it rallies to form a third peak. Then it reacts again. By now, it has used up much of the demand existing at the two previous lows, and it pushes down through. Volume may be high on the first peak, and is apt to be relatively low on the second and third peaks—picking up, however, when the direction of the new major move has been set.

FIGURE 25

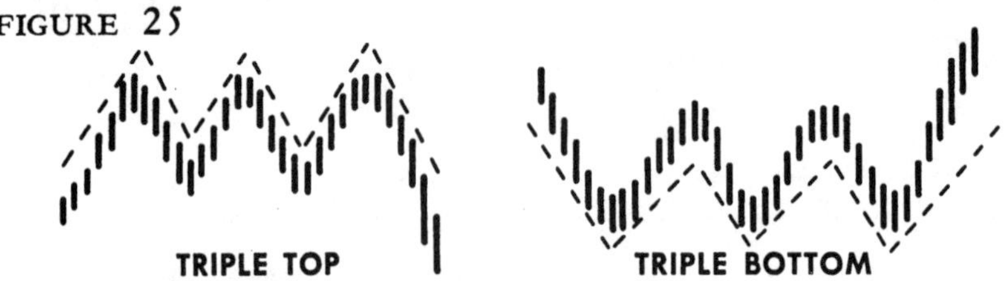

MARKET TACTICS

The conservative chart reader will await the completion of a pattern before taking a position. Those more speculatively inclined may try to anticipate, and thus "sell at the top and buy at the bottom." Proceed at your own risk.

There are several cautions to be observed. For one

thing, the trader should not expect a *small pattern*—that is, one that has taken form in a short time—to support a *big move*. And, as we indicated at the outset, the Double Top or Bottom is a tough one to anticipate, even for the most experienced chartists. A favorable answer to the following questions will minimize the risk:

1. Did the price decline about 5% or more from the first peak?
2. Was there unusual volume around the first peak?
3. Does the chart history of the stock designate this area as a likely major turning point, where, for example, long-range support or resistance is to be expected, or have major trendlines been broken?
4. Is the general market in a downtrend, or at least neutral?

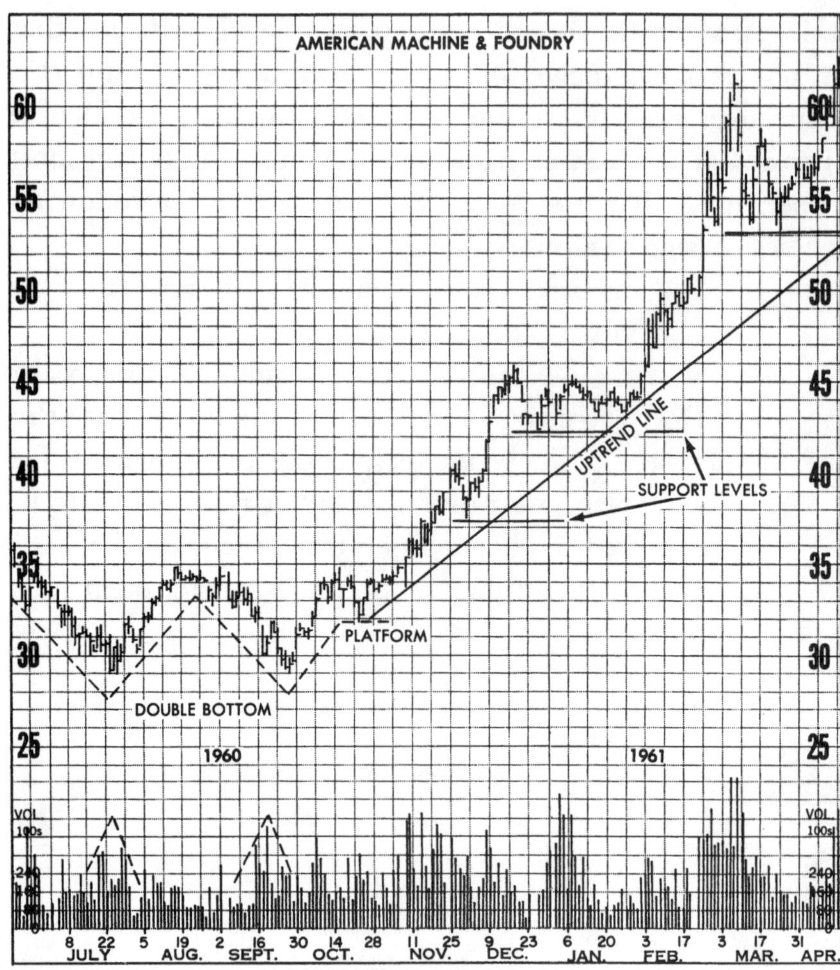

PLATE 15 AMERICAN MACHINE & FOUNDRY— Double Bottom With Platform

AMF is another perfect example of a Double Bottom formation with a little platform extension. Volume tended to expand slightly around each of the two bottoms and then pick up noticeably on the rally from the platform, which in effect completed the pattern. Throughout the 66 point advance, neither the major trendline nor any support line was violated. Of further interest is the fact that in May, 1961. (not shown) prices broke the trendline and the 107 support line and then continued to decline. By the end of the year, most of the advance from the 70 breakout had been completely retraced. (When the reader finishes this book, a close re-analysis of this chart will show up other formations not outlined nor covered through this Chapter—a Measured Move, a Wedge and a Head & Shoulders failure.)

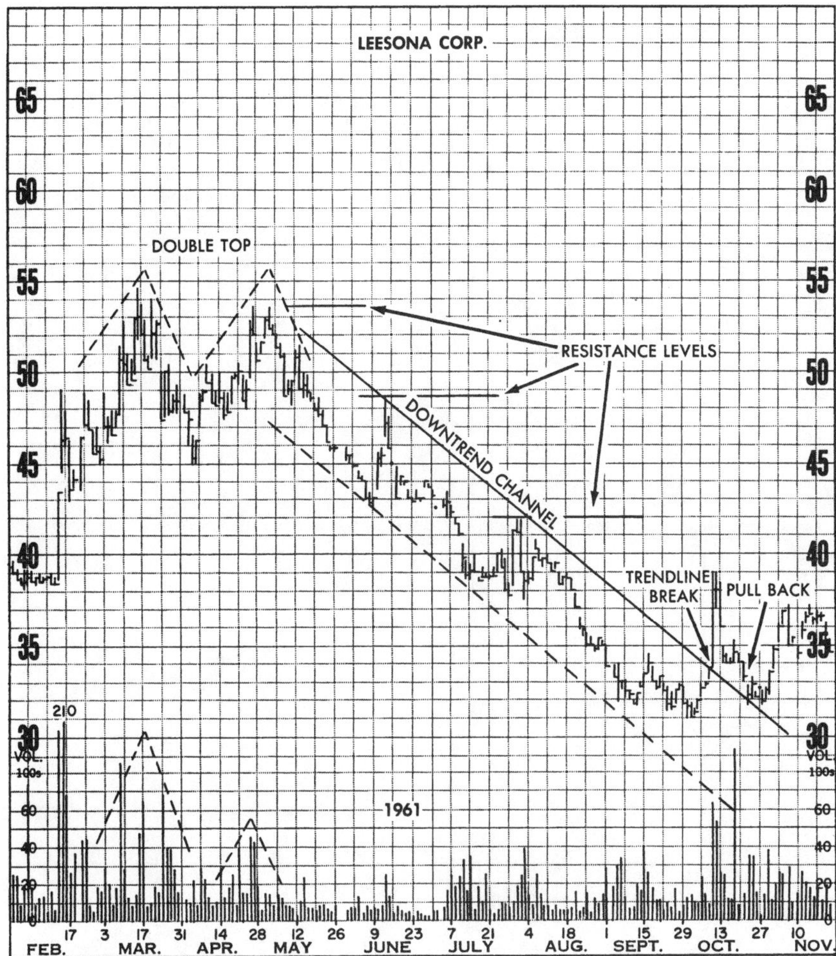

PLATE 16 LEESONA — Double Top

The first top made in March was the culmination of an advance from 33 in December. The rally back to the high in April was on light volume, which did not augur well for a breakthrough into new high ground. As the level of the first top (54⅝) was approached, volume increased and the advance was thrown back. Evidently, the supply of stock for sale at that level was too much for the demand, and hence a Double Top was completed when the decline extended beyond the $45 level. Subsequently, prices retraced all the ground won in the previous advance. The Downtrend channel is outlined; attention is directed to the trendline-breaking rally in October and the magnetic pull-back to the trendline, an effect described in Chapter 2. Also notice that resistance levels established during the decline were never violated.

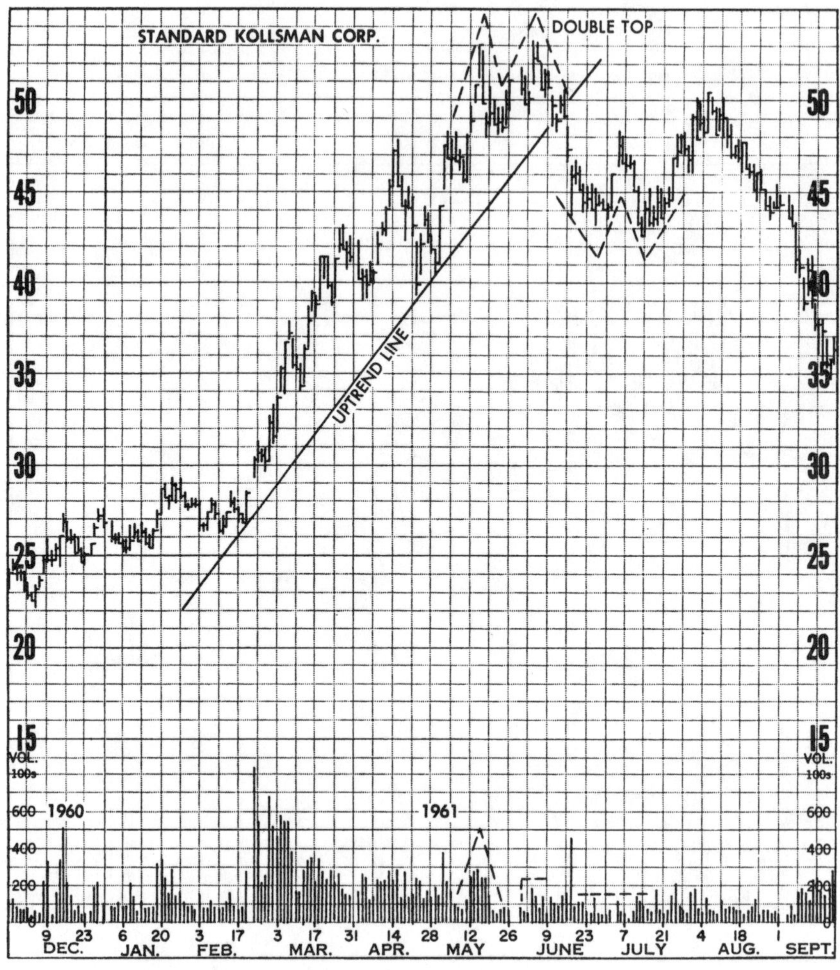

PLATE 17 STANDARD KOLLSMAN — Double Top

The Double Top that formed in May and June is especially interesting, because right after it was completed, prices formed what appeared to be a Double Bottom. The rally from this unusual counter-balancing formation challenged the Double Top, but fell short, and the interrupted decline from the highs was renewed. Analysis of both of these formations should consider that the valid Double Top took shape after a long advance, and the completion of the top also broke a major uptrend line. Volume was heavy on the first top and light on the second top. The second formation—the potential double bottom took shape at a very unlikely level for a Double Bottom. Volume was light on both bottoms and the subsequent rally did not violate any other significant chart point. This Double Top would have caused the chartist some anxious moments, but eventually proved to have been a valid signal, (By February, 1962, the price of this stock was under 29.)

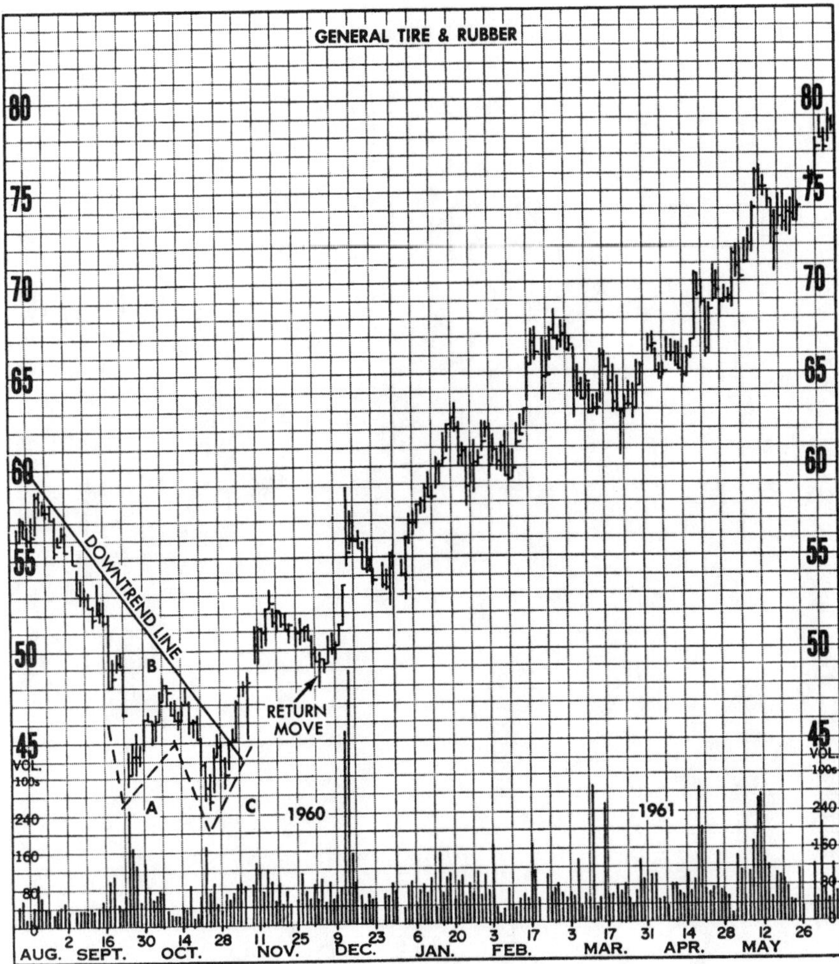

PLATE 18 GENERAL TIRE — Double Bottom Variation

It was difficult—but not impossible—to identify this Double Bottom formation before prices in November rallied over the October highs (B) to complete the pattern. The second bottom (C) was more than a point lower than the first (A), and this could have caused uncertainty. In a great majority of Double Bottoms, the second bottom is slightly higher than the first, but quite a few behave like this one. As noted in this chapter, "Heavy volume around one or both peaks or lows (in the case of bottoms) tends to confirm the development of a Double Top or Bottom." This was the first clue. The second clue was the rally in the first week of November which broke the downtrend line drawn along the previous highs. Then, of course, the continuing rally above B completed the bottom. Since the rally from C carried well above the level of B, we regard the reaction to that level as a return move.

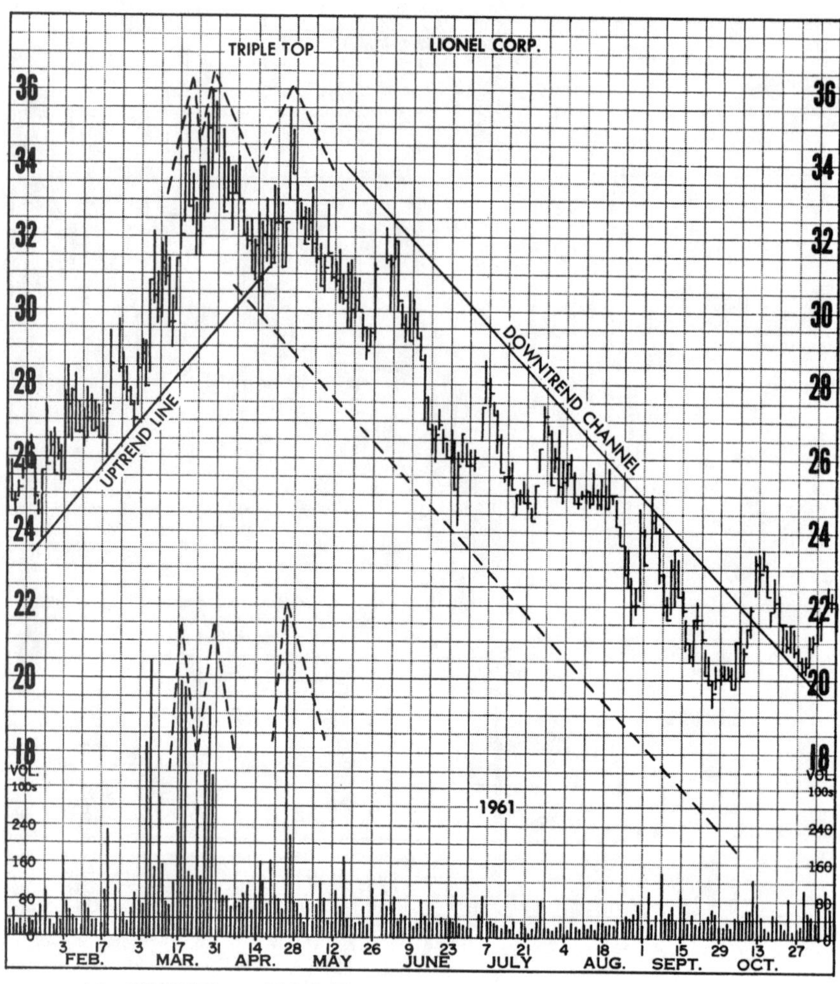

PLATE 19 LIONEL — Triple Top

On March 21, Lionel reached an all time high of 35½ but closed below the previous close marking a Reversal Day (see Chapter 11). Six trading days later, prices touched a new high of 35⅞, only ⅜ above the Reversal Day high. Four weeks later, a third attempt at a new high was stopped at 35½. Each high was made on unusually high volume and the net effect was a Triple Top. The foregoing chapter indicated that Triple Tops were rare and have been classified as a variation of the common Double Top. In fact, the first two tops looked like a clear Double Top, and the chartist who followed this pattern would have been shaken when he saw prices rally for a third attempt at new highs. He would have had to hold his ground unless the third rally were successful in overcoming the previous highs. The ensuing downtrend followed a trendline fairly closely until October.

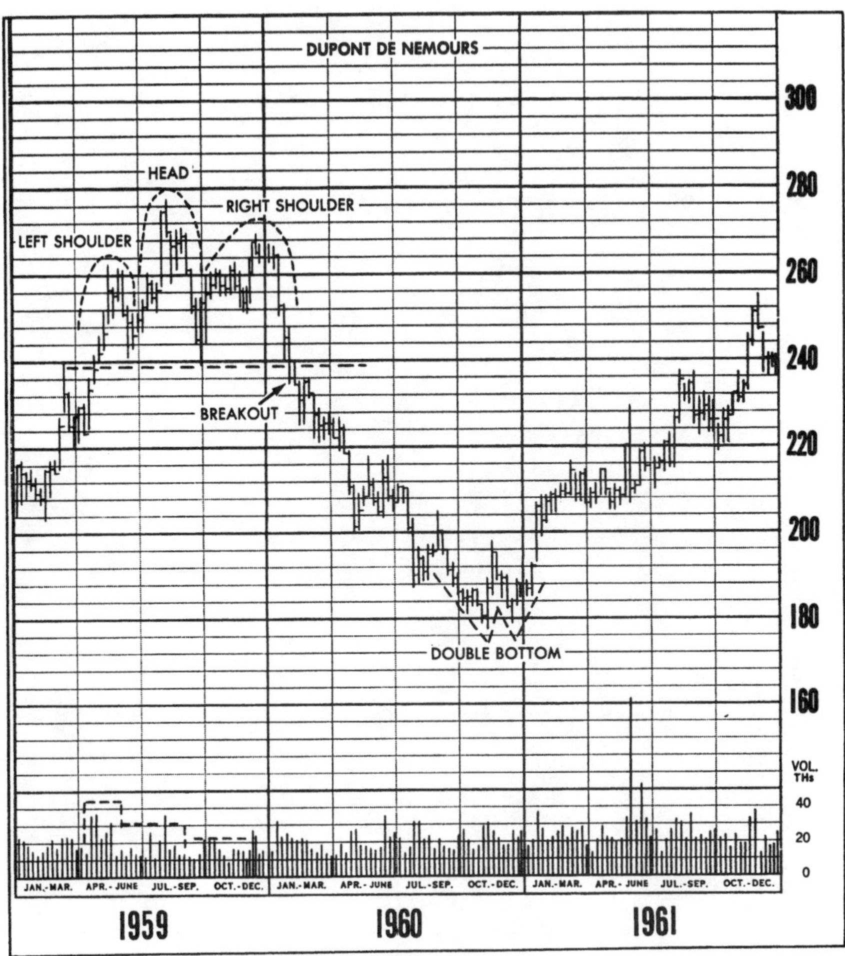

PLATE 20 du PONT (Weekly Range Chart) — Double Bottom

The du Pont chart above is the second illustration of how weekly, high, low and close charts form the same kind of patterns as the daily charts. The Double Bottom that formed in late 1960 reversed a decline of approximately 100 points, or $100 a share. (This may be a little shocking to those of the "uninitiated public" who never understand how a "blue chip" can go down, and du Pont is the "bluest of the blue".) At around 177, buying rallied the stock 20 points and then prices declined all the way back to test the 177 level. Demand again increased just above the 177 level, and this next rally carried over the previous rally high, thus completing a Double Bottom reversal. A glance at the 1959 top will reveal an outlined Head & Shoulders Top (with only the return move to the neckline missing). Both the price and volume pattern were typical and this chart could have appeared as an illustration in the preceding chapter.

LINE AND SAUCER FORMATIONS

Lines and Saucers form the chart reader's dream patterns. They're easy to recognize, they're reliable, they usually portend an extensive price move and—best of all—they give the chartist plenty of time to assume a market position close to the bottom or top of the ensuing swing. They have only one major drawback: they're rare among popular, actively traded stocks.

When a *Line Formation* evolves into a major bottom, it is commonly called a *long base*. This appears on the chart as a long sideways movement of prices within a narrow range, followed by a sudden eruption into new high ground, well above the preceding price range. Sometimes, although rarely, a line formation will form a *major top*, in which case it will look like one of our Western mesas, or plateaus.

FIGURE 26

Breakout

Breakout

LINE BOTTOM OR LONG BASE

LINE TOP

The *Saucer,* or "rounding turn," is closely related to the Line Formation, but has its own characteristics and may form much more quickly. (See Figure 27.) Prices forming a saucer gradually curve upward (in the case of a *bottom* formation) or downward (in the case of a *top*). The curve, of course, tips off the probable direction of the major move to come. There's another picturesque feature. A great majority of Saucers (not quite all) develop a *Handle* or *Platform,* consisting of either a horizontal or slanted line, before the main move gets underway. Perhaps the formation should be called a *Saucepan,* instead.

FIGURE 27

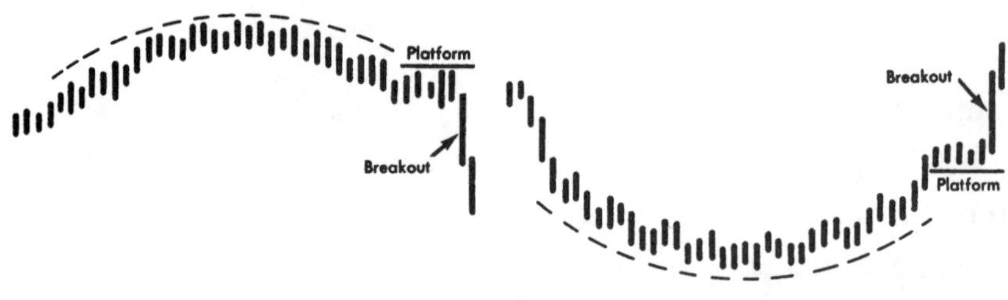

SAUCER TOP **SAUCER BOTTOM**

HOW IT HAPPENS

As with all valid chart patterns, these stem from typical market psychology in certain situations. For example, the Line Bottom, or "long base," occurs when the supply of and demand for a stock are in a very stable balance. There is little trading in the stock, because there has been no change in its outlook, for better or worse, and no news to draw attention to it. Stockholders see little reason to sell at the current price level, and potential buyers see little reason to buy, especially if they must bid the price up to smoke out any sellers. A breakout from this long base on increased volume probably means that something is brewing—a new product, a jump in sales or profits, a merger—and this rumor or fact has produced an unusual demand for the stock. Incidentally, such breakouts are rarely accompanied by company announcements—those come later. Frequently, "insiders" have been quietly adding to their holdings during the "long base" period. At any rate, someone in the know is buying, and sooner or later, the facts become known to more and more people, and the price begins to take off.

VOLUME

A tidy characteristic of the Line and Saucer formations is that the *volume* portion of the chart tends to follow the *price*. Throughout a Line, or base formation, volume is always exceptionally low—until the breakout into new high ground. Even then, trading may be relatively light at the outset, but it soon expands dramatically.

In a typical Saucer, on the other hand, trading slowly dimishes to a low at the turn of the formation, then gradually picks up as prices curve to complete the pattern or move to the Platform stage. Volume thus has formed a saucer itself. It may become quite active at the start of the Platform, and again at the end, as the stock breaks out of the Platform area.

At the outset, we noted that the Line and Saucer formations were easily recognizable, and we have discussed how to recognize them. Now, a mild word of caution. One should *never* take a pattern of any kind for granted *until it is nearly completed*. This applies even to so simple a formation as the Line, or long base. A stock may appear to be developing one, but evolve into an entirely different formation in short order.

There is an interesting variation of the base formation that deserves comment. On occasion, just before the breakout move, there will be a "shakeout,"—that is, a false swing in the opposite direction, which may "shake out" timid or ill-informed stockholders. (See Figure 28.) During this shakeout prices drop to a new low. Then they rally through the base range and into new high ground, on high volume. Despite the weakness displayed by the brief dip, this variation can result in as great a rally as the more orthodox base formation.

FIGURE 28

LONG BASE WITH "SHAKE-OUT" MOVE

MARKET TACTICS

Our "dream formations" unfortunately, do not often occur among popular or active issues. The Line or Saucer is more apt to take shape on the charts of stocks in which trading is light and on which little information is available to the general public. On the other hand, the profit potential in following such a pattern is great, and the risk can be held to a minimum. Hence, it behooves the investor-analyst to maintain an adequate collection of charts, and keep an eye peeled for Lines and Saucers.

The best time to buy a stock that has formed a long base is as soon as possible after the breakout. True, as in breakouts from all formations, there is often a kickback, or return move to the base, before the advance really gets into high gear. (See Figure 29.) But the advance from this type of formation is so steep that one who hesitates may miss the bus.

FIGURE 29

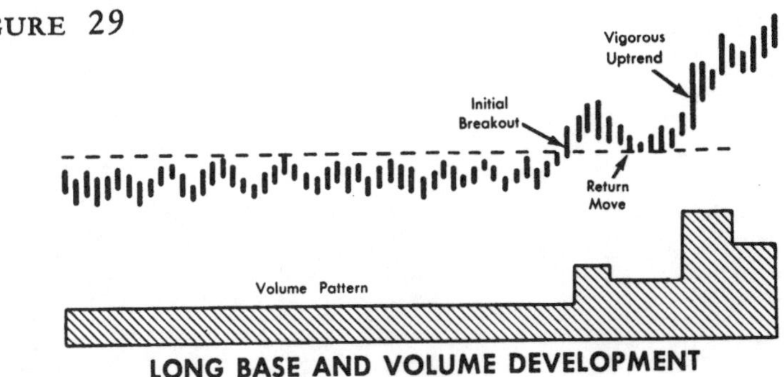

LONG BASE AND VOLUME DEVELOPMENT

One has more time to take a position when a stock is forming a Saucer bottom. In fact, there are four favorable times to buy: (1) During the upcurve, when volume and prices are gradually rising; (2) At the end of the curve, when a purchase may be made if the stock begins to level off on reduced volume—but it's hard to anticipate the precise end of the curve; (3) During the formation of the platform, preferably at the low point of the Platform's trading range; (4) On the actual breakout from the Platform.

FIGURE 30

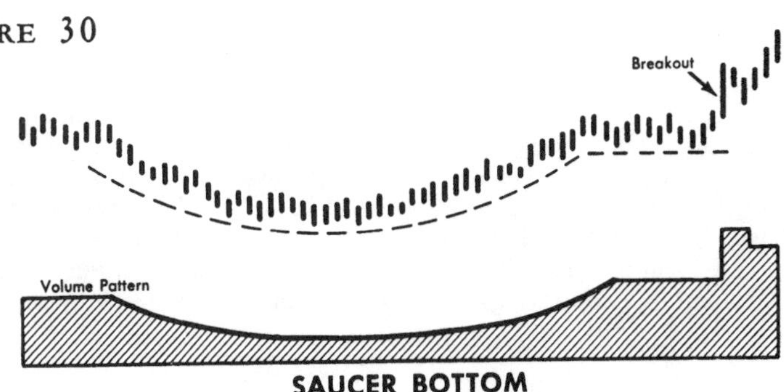

SAUCER BOTTOM

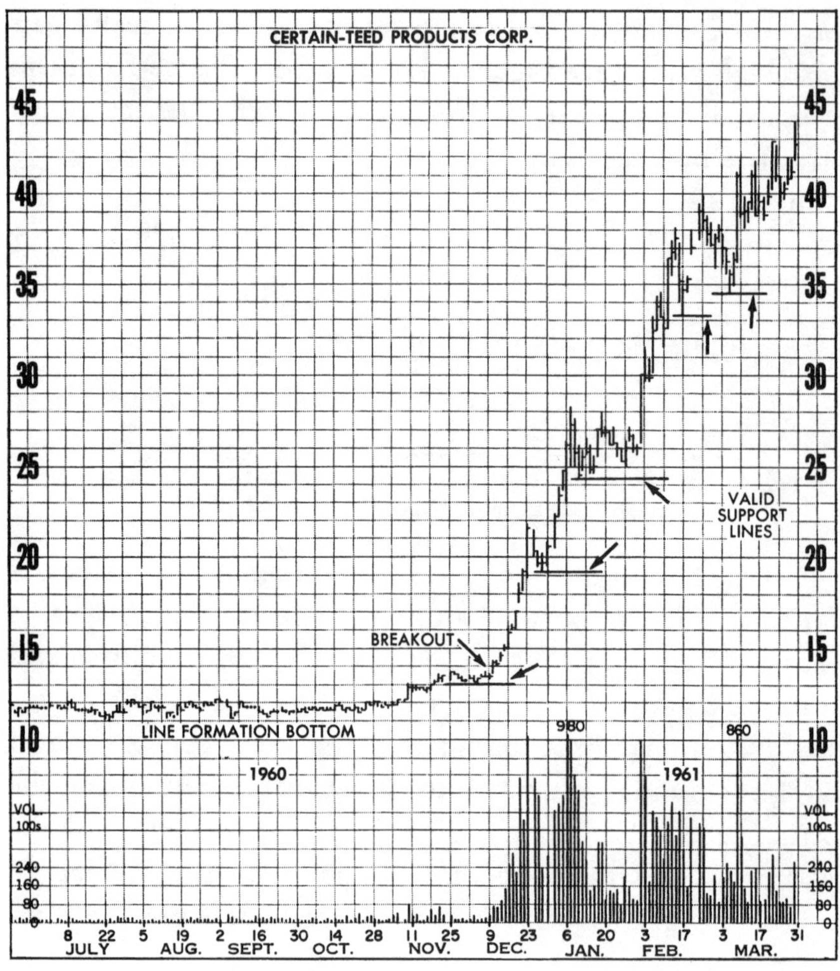

PLATE 21 CERTAIN-TEED — Line Bottom or "Long Base"

This chart was chosen to portray an unusually long base and almost complete lack of activity. If the chart were long enough, it would show this line formation extending back several years. Prices and volume curved out of the base together. The old saw "the longer the base, the bigger the move" is validated here. This move, which began quietly in November at a price of about 13, reached 44 by the end of the chart, March 31, and hit 64 by May. For those keeping score on the times that charts perform as expected and the times they don't, it is interesting to point out that not one valid support level (horizontal lines marked) was violated throughout the advance.

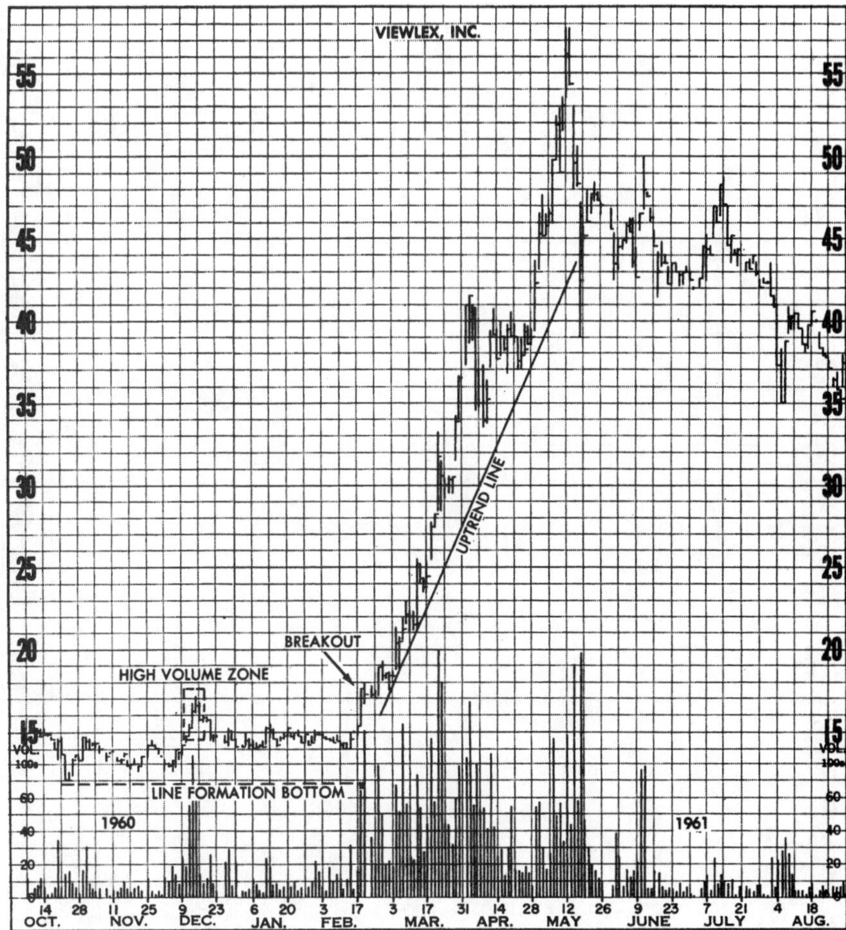

PLATE 22 VIEWLEX — Line Bottom

Although this base was not really completed until late February, when prices moved to new highs on very high volume, an earlier rally on a burst of volume in December flashed a bull signal well in advance of the big move. Many of the great "bull" moves studied in the past 10 years were similarly signaled in advance. Watch for this volume signal in any stock that is basically moving sideways on light volume. The flareup in volume tells the technician that something big is brewing; the failure of a follow-through means that the brew is not ready yet. A two-to-six month wait for the big move is not uncommon. This volume signal, called a "high volume zone" in Chapter 3, can also pinpoint a potent resistance level which, when overcome, can set the advance in high gear. (After reading Chapter 11, you can identify the top as a Two Day Reversal.)

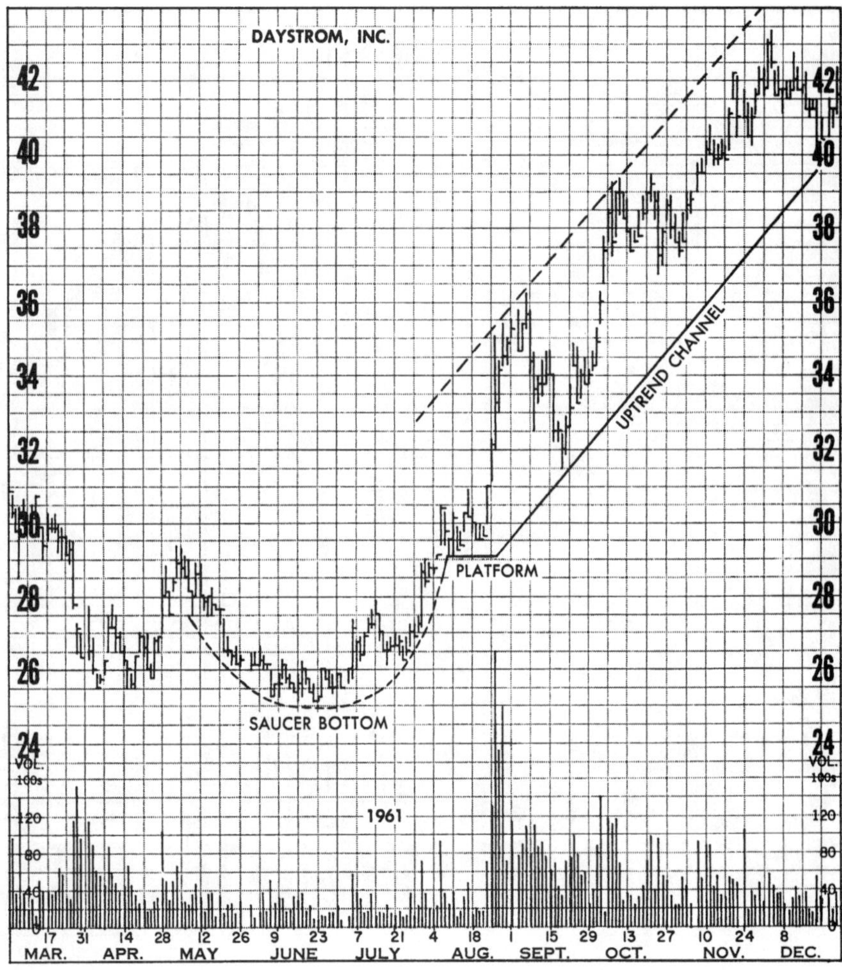

PLATE 23 DAYSTROM — Saucer Bottom

The Saucer Bottom found in May, June and July looks more like a cup with a handle. Prices rounded the bottom and the volume pattern followed the same shaped pattern. There was a slight irregularity in the shape of the saucer in July, but the volume pattern remained steady. The breakout from the platform saw volume explode, and it remained relatively high throughout the upmove. Readers may wish to refer to this chart again after finishing this book. They may note an interesting chart development in August and September. A tight upslanting—but incomplete—Flag, normally one of the most reliable of all "bull" formations, took shape in late August but broke down, only to form a small Head & Shoulders bottom. This in turn led to a regular Flag in October and November.

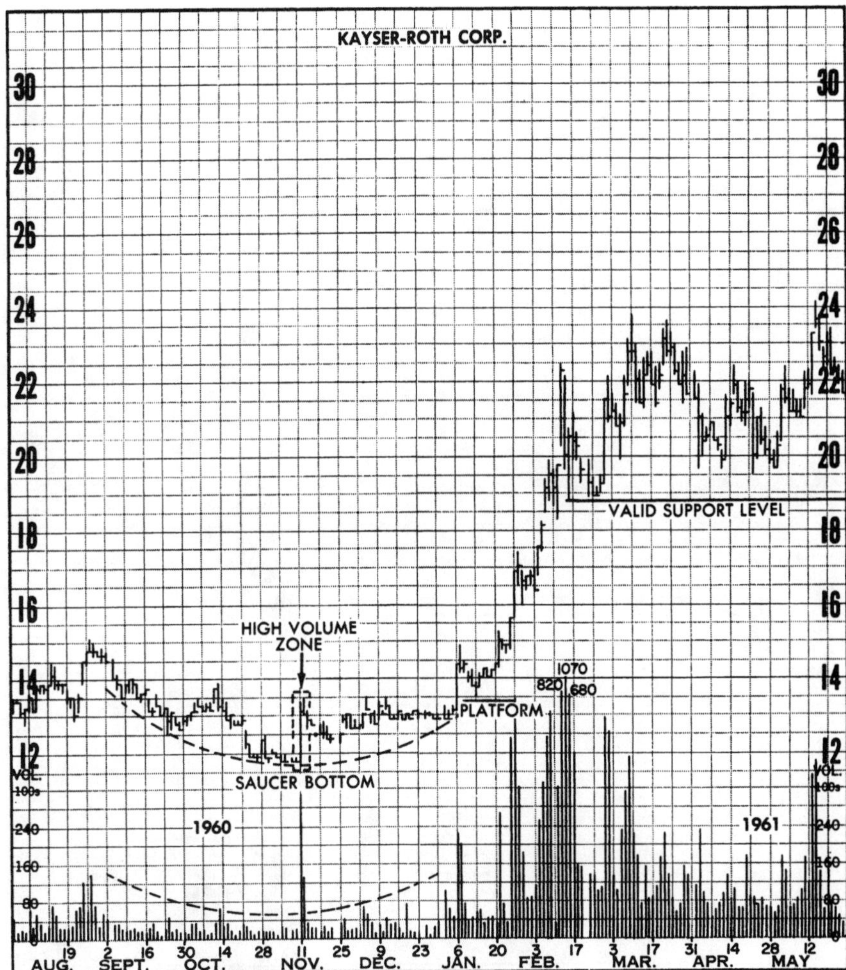

PLATE 24 KAYSER-ROTH — Saucer Bottom

This Saucer or Rounding Bottom is punctuated smack in the middle by a two-day rally on high volume. The area of that flash of volume is outlined as a high volume zone where an unusual change in stock ownership occurred. Presumably, if prices later rise above this area, the market will be in a good position to extend its advance. Those who bought in the zone would have profits and a rally would indicate that the supply of stock available above the zone was diminished. It can also be regarded as a preliminary signal similar to the one described in the Viewlex analysis. At any rate, this volume zone occurred within a major base pattern. A small platform formed just above the volume zone, and the subsequent advance was on very high volume, thus fulfilling all of the expectations of this type of chart development.

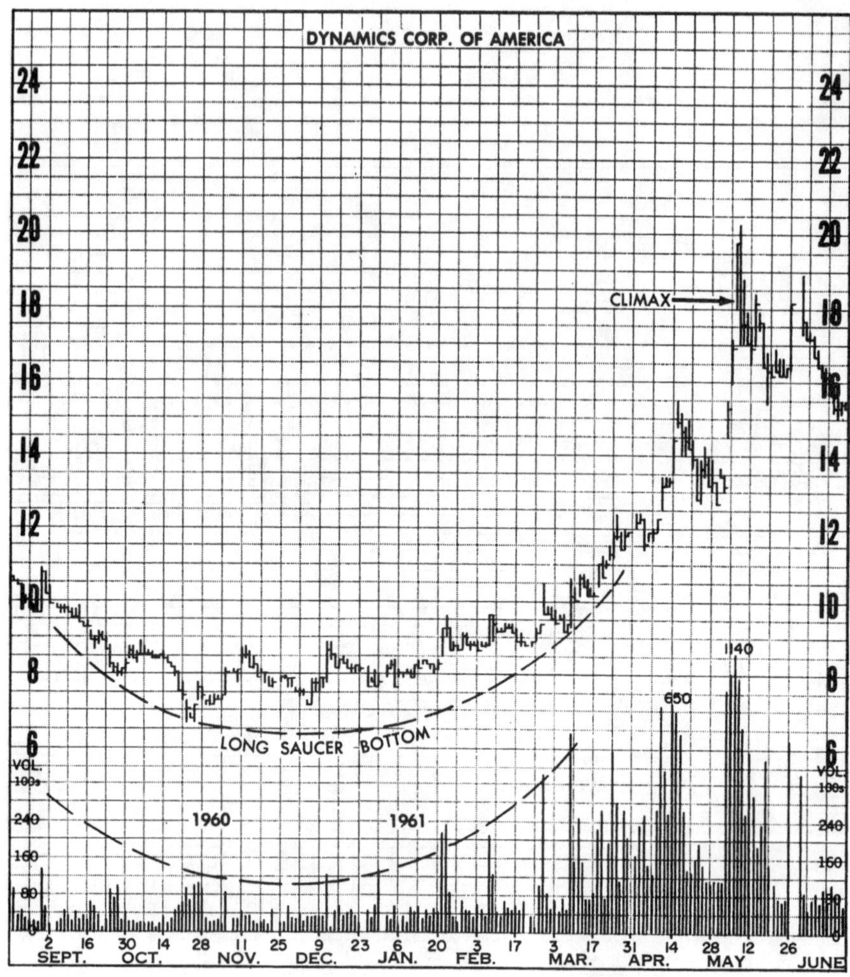

PLATE 25 DYNAMICS CORP. — Long Saucer Bottom

Although this saucer took more than seven months to form, the long wait proved quite worthwhile. Prices tripled from bottom to top, and doubled in an eight week period beginning in March. Volume remained low throughout the rounding process and then expanded as the advance became spirited. There wasn't any platform or handle on this saucer, which distinguishes it from the previous two examples. Unlike line formations, which always take considerable time to form, saucers usually form in much shorter periods. This is one of the longer blooming varieties.

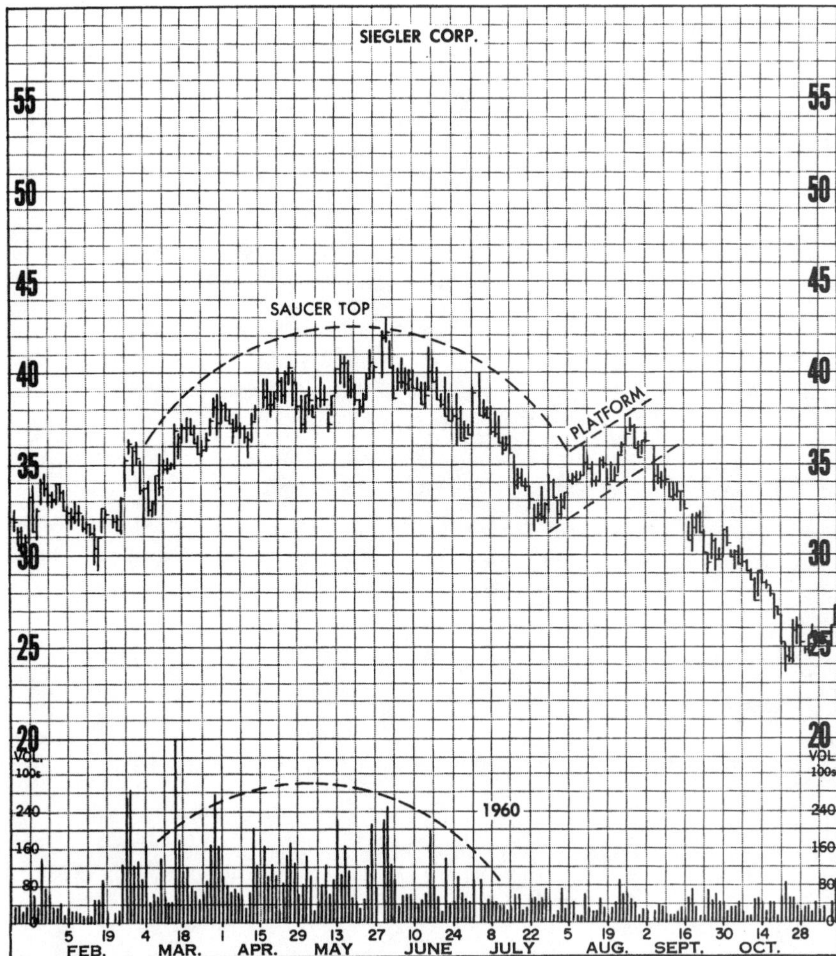

PLATE 26 SIEGLER — Saucer Top

Except for a two day flare-up to new highs on volume in June, this pattern is a classic Saucer Top. Even so, the rounding turn and the platform or handle leave little to the imagination. The volume pattern is especially interesting since it nearly outlines the Saucer Top by itself. Saucer Tops often show such a volume pattern, but can also form with diminishing volume at the peak (an inverted volume pattern). It is rare to find a Saucer Bottom, however, in which the volume does not follow the price pattern.

V FORMATIONS

In the stock market, as elsewhere, where there is profit, there is risk. And, generally speaking, the greater the potential profit, the greater the risk. So it is with a certain group of chart reversal patterns which are so powerful that they spark the most dynamic of all price swings—but, unfortunately, are among the hardest to anticipate or analyze. In fact, even after they are completed, the most experienced chartist can't be certain that trends will follow through in a normal way. These elusive chart patterns are known as V Formations.

In other reversal patterns, buyers and sellers vie for dominance over a more or less extended period, with one group and then the other alternating in the lead. This interplay of forces may be said to prepare the market for a reversal—and to alert the chartist. Not so with a V Formation. As the name implies, there is no such preparation. The *progressive* shift from a downtrend to an uptrend, which is a function of other reversal patterns, is absent.

Instead, the V-turn strikes with little warning; it's dramatic and final. It's as though, by some prearranged signal, all the stock that sellers have to offer has been suddenly taken up, and buyers remain the dominant force for some time to come.

Hence, V Formations signal sharp reversals in trend, but at the same time are among the most difficult to analyze. Nevertheless, there are a few positive clues that can be of assistance in catching a good number of these moves. And because the price swings that follow are often substantial, it pays to master these patterns. At the end of this chapter, we will carefully examine a number of actual market situations in an effort to lessen the mystery.

But first, let us define our V patterns. There are two kinds: the *True V* and the *Extended V*.

THE TRUE V FORMATION

The typical true V (Figure 31) is V-shaped indeed, and has three components:

A. *Downtrend:* More often than not, the decline that marks the left arm of a V is fairly sharp and extensive, but it may be quite slow and irregular—just so the trend is down.

B. *Pivot:* A single day's action frequently marks the low point of the decline. At times, the turn is more gradual, but rarely does the price pause in this region for more than a few days. In most instances, volume picks up noticeably near the lows. Sometimes, the heaviest volume will be registered on the very day of the turning point, marking this as a *climax day*.

C. *Uptrend:* The first signal of a turn is given when

the stock price penetrates a downtrend line, which has been drawn along the rally peaks of the preceding decline. After the turn, volume tends to pick up gradually as the move progresses. The early part of this phase is the trouble spot, because until the move has gone far enough, we can't be sure that the formation is a valid V-turn. However, the uptrend phase of the true V will tend to duplicate the preceding downtrend leg. If the downtrend, A, measures down as a 45 degree angle, the uptrend, C, is likely to measure up as a 45 degree angle.

FIGURE 31

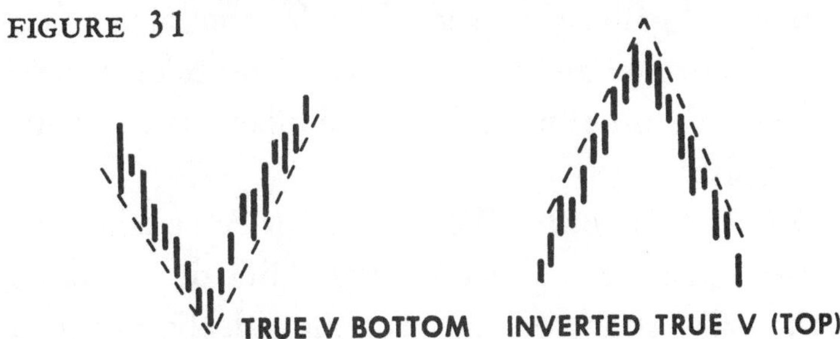

INVERTED TRUE V

The *Inverted True V* marks a top and is, as its name indicates, the opposite of the V bottom. In a great majority of cases, volume picks up sharply around the pivot, and this forms an upside-down V on the volume scale, as well as the price. Sometimes, however, volume on the turn is relatively normal or even unusually light.

THE EXTENDED V FORMATION

No less potent than the True V, the Extended V (Figure 32) lends itself more readily to accurate forecasting because of one significant difference. This comes after the pivot, when the stock has penetrated up through the downtrend line, as described just above. In the True V, the upward move begins more or less immediately. In the Extended V, a fairly sizable lateral trading range develops. Eventually, the stock breaks out above the tops of this trading range, thus completing the formation. In detail, the four components of an Extended V are:

A. *Downtrend:* As in the True V, this may be steep or irregular. In a good many cases—though far from all—the downtrend is interrupted by a "sideways" or "consolidation" phase a short distance before the final low.

B. *Pivot:* Again as in the True V, the turn often comes in a single day, but sometimes takes several days. Volume behavior is similar: usually up sharply.

C. *Initial Markup:* The stock price pushes up through either (1) a downtrend line drawn along the rally peaks of the preceding decline or (2) a line marking the top of the "sideways" or "consolidation" phase that formed just before the pivot. Volume picks up during this penetration.

D. *Platform:* This is the portion that sets the Extended V apart from the True V, and makes it more identifiable, as well. The Platform may be quite horizontal, but usually slants moderately down. As the platform is developing, volume tends to slacken. Then, when the stock begins its final swing toward the breakout, volume tends to pick up. The breakout itself normally is accompanied by heavy volume.

FIGURE 32

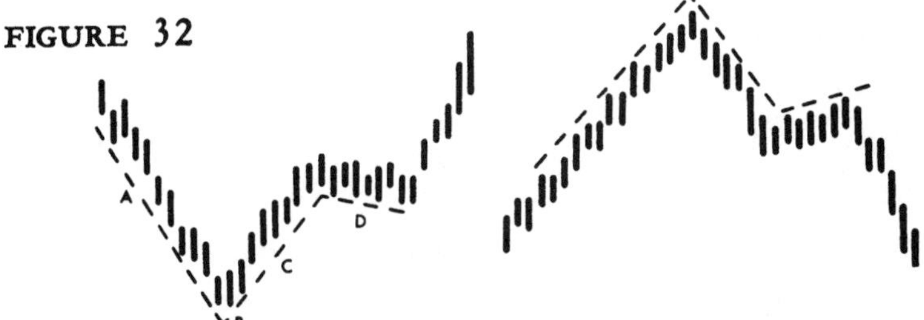

EXTENDED V (BOTTOM) INVERTED EXTENDED V (TOP)

An Extended V may be regarded as completed, or confirmed, when the price breaks through the highs of the Platform on increased volume. If the Platform happens to slant downward, one may watch for the stock to push through the downtrend line drawn along the rally peaks within the Platform. If this penetration occurs on increased volume, the pattern is likely to follow through, and a trader may at this point decide to buy near the bottom of an extended swing.

LEFTHANDED

Sometimes an Extended V develops in which the price and volume follow exactly the pattern described above, except that the Platform is on the left instead of the right. Some people are born with the appendix on the left and the heart pointed right; it doesn't seem to matter. The Lefthanded V spells a price reversal just the same.

FIGURE 33

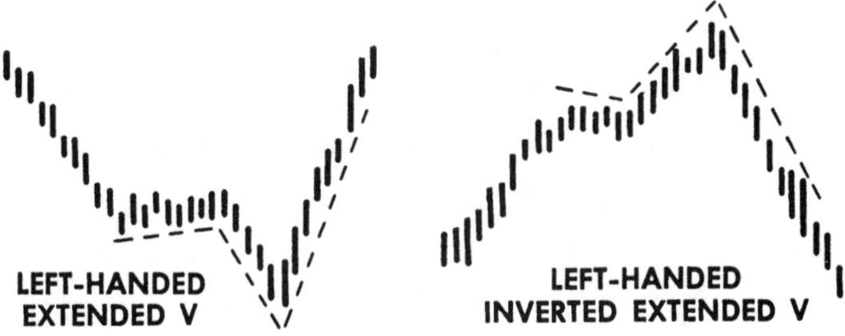

LEFT-HANDED EXTENDED V

LEFT-HANDED INVERTED EXTENDED V

It's a good thing to learn the probabilities, or odds, and act accordingly. It's a bad thing to take a little information on market behavior or mathematics and turn it into a rigid "system," which one follows blindly—as long as the money holds out. It is always necessary to be flexible and imaginative in applying what one knows to actual market situations.

Nowhere is this more true than in the case of the V Formations, which we described at the outset as among the hardest to anticipate or analyze. We did not mean to imply they were *impossible,* for if they were, it would be a waste of time to discuss them. But the trader confronting a possible V turn should be alert for false signals, aware of the pitfalls, conscious of the risk as well as the potential profit, and ready to beat a retreat in a hurry.

The need for a flexible approach is suggested by the way V Formations tend to occur. Every actively traded stock has a mixed following: in-and-out traders, informed investors and the general public. In nearly all chart patterns, the interplay of all three groups may be seen—but not in V turns. These are generally the product of a dramatic switch in market psychology, resulting from some surprise development, unforseen even by the informed investors. (These are rarely so well-informed that they buy stock at the very bottom of a downtrend; they are more likely to "accumulate" it on the decline.)

An *unexpected* news item, a political development, or even a broadcaster's tip can cause a wave of orders to flow into brokerage offices and suddenly reverse a stock trend. Such a reversal, by definition, is impossible to foresee.

One exception occurs when there is a large block of

stock to be sold. Here, the supply is let out cautiously but steadily, creating constant pressure on the price structure. Once the supply is gone, the price tends to snap back like a rubber band.

In any case, the chartist-investor must watch for the V to be completed and study the past of the stock and the nature of the immediate situation to determine the probable extent of the subsequent swing, and then act—with care.

It is safer for beginners (and perhaps experienced operators as well) to make a number of "dry runs" in V situations before putting any money down. In analysis, there is no substitute for practice. On the following pages, we offer a number of case histories, posing a variety of problems. The hope is that they will emphasize the need for flexibility, and add to the experience necessary to cope with the tricky, but rewarding, V turn.

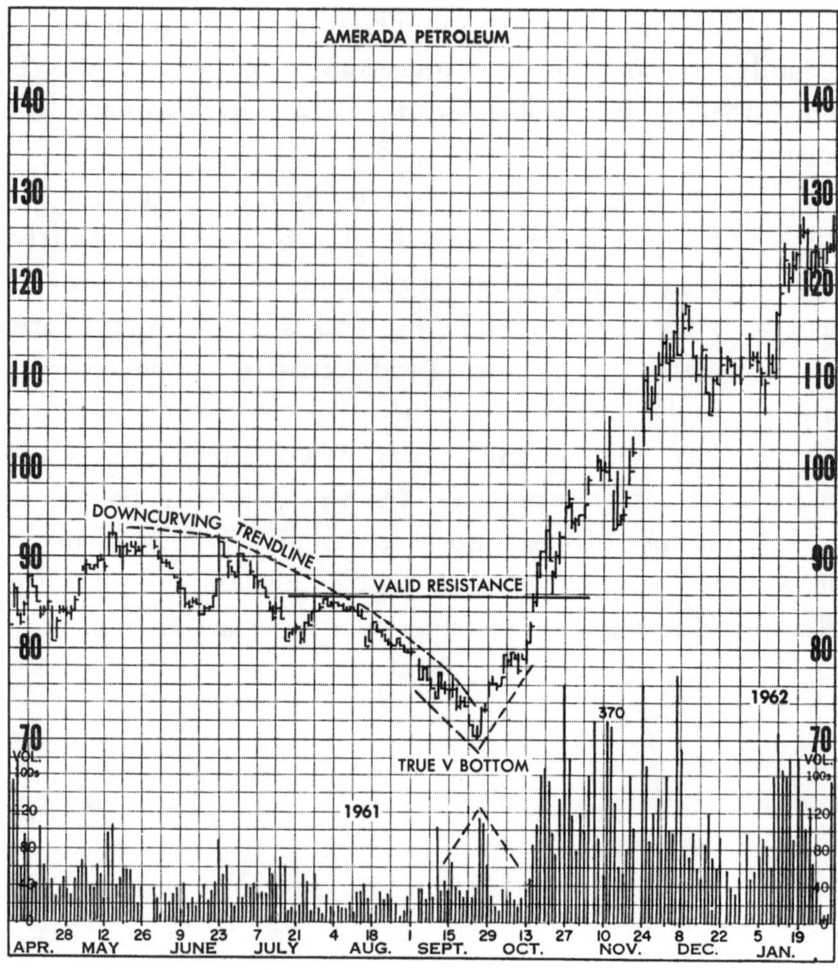

PLATE 27 AMERADA — True V Formation

The true V outlined above sparked an advance of 50 points in eleven weeks. What was more remarkable was the fact that the market averages were in the doldrums and market breadth studies showed that most stocks were in downtrends. Anyone following price movements in September, 1961, might have been lucky enough to catch this turn close to the bottom. The clues were the breaking of a downcurving trendline on high volume with a small breakaway gap (see Chapter 11). Because V formations are not easy to identify one probably would have to wait until the price topped 80, when the tremendous increase in volume left little doubt that a true V formation had been completed.

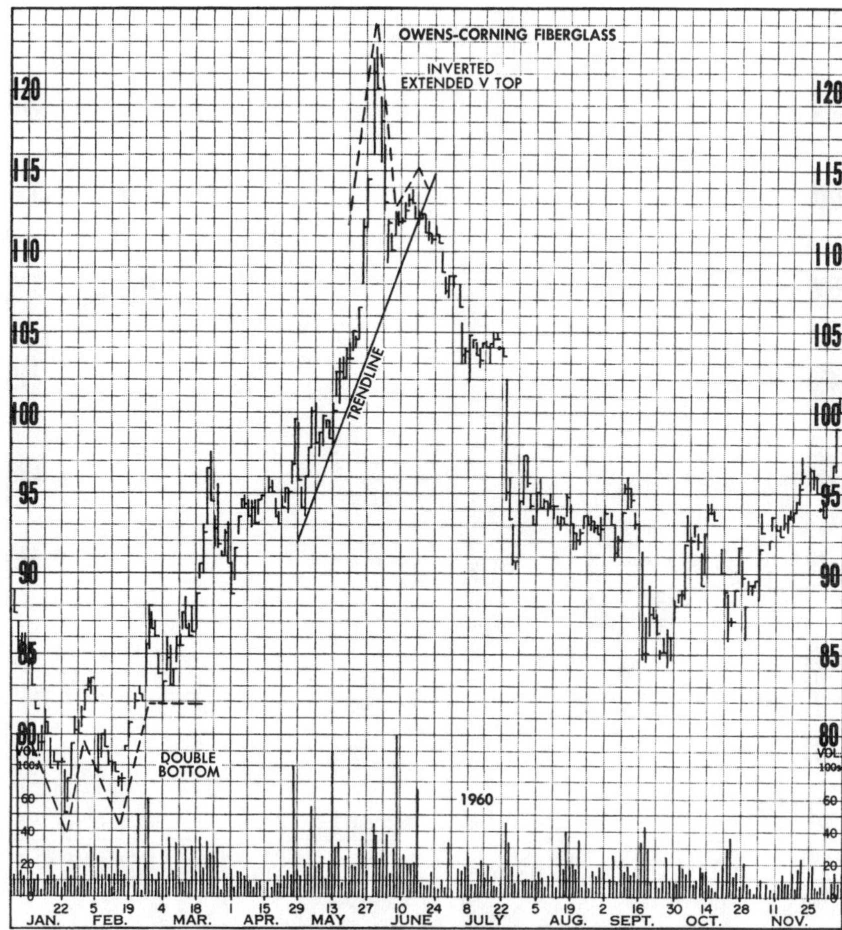

PLATE 28 OWENS-CORNING — Inverted Extended V

The top formation that occurred in May and June of 1960, in some quarters would be called a "church steeple", however, it fits nicely into this book's category of the Inverted Extended V. Notice how the platform, or extension part of the formation, followed the sharp trendline drawn along the lows of the advance that preceded the actual top. The breaking of this trendline completed the top, but the chartist would be wise to wait for the breaking of the reaction low at 109¼. Incidentally, except for the trendline mentioned, the discerning chartist will note that Owens-Corning in 1960 did not particularly favor trendline development. The uptrend from February and downtrend from June on did not conform to straight lines. On the other hand, the chart did conform beautifully to support and resistance principles and other formations, such as the Double Bottom in January and February. All stocks have their own chart characteristics, which should be studied carefully in every analysis.

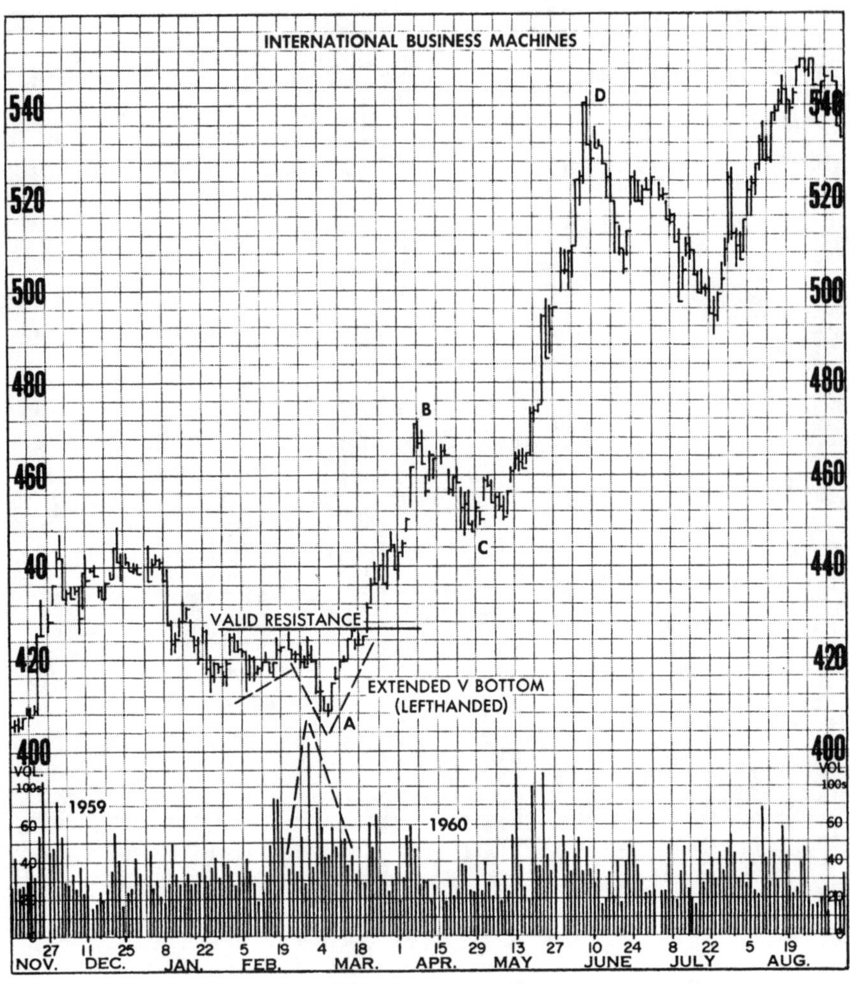

PLATE 29 IBM — Extended V Bottom (Left-Handed)

No chart analysis would be worth its salt without a look at the high-priced but ever popular International Business Machines. It can be seen that this legend of American business and the stock market still conforms to rather normal chart development. The Extended V Bottom (left handed) formed at a previous support zone (congestion in October-November, 1959) and set the stage for a rise of about 134 points. Note the heavy volume around the bottom which tells the chartist that an important change of ownership is occurring. The formation is confirmed when prices carry over what should have been a resistance level (the February highs). After finishing Chapter 8, you will be able to analyze a measured move formation which overshot its mark (C to D was greater than A to B). Another formation of interest is the Pennant in November, which turned into a downside breakout from an Ascending Triangle.

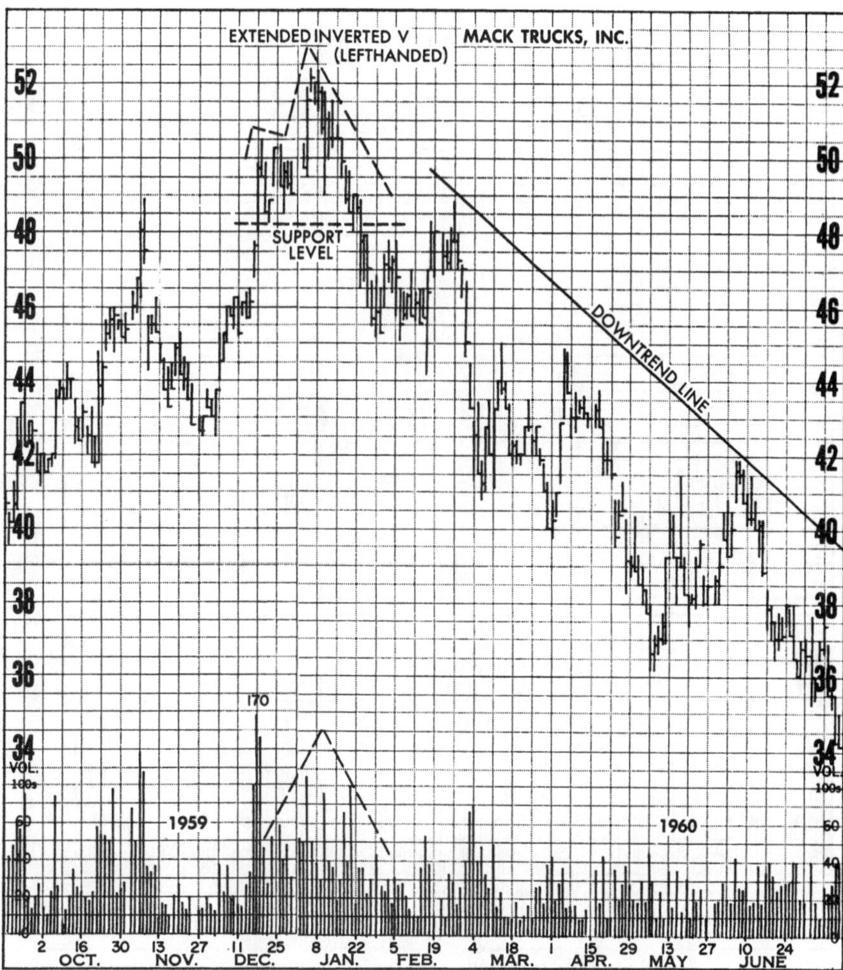

PLATE 30 MACK TRUCKS — Inverted Extended V (Left Handed)

The left-handed type of extended V top (or, as labeled above and in the preceding chapter, the extended inverted V) is more difficult to anticipate than the right-handed type. This is especially so in the Mack Truck chart above. The platform on the left side takes a triangular shape, and the analyst must await the breaking of the lowest point of the triangle before assuming that a V top has been completed. In most cases the platform, whether on the left or right side, is fairly well outlined, so that when prices break through the bottom of the range (on V tops), the analyst can complete his analysis of the V reversal pattern. On this chart, the major downtrend line held intact despite some rather wide swings on the way down.

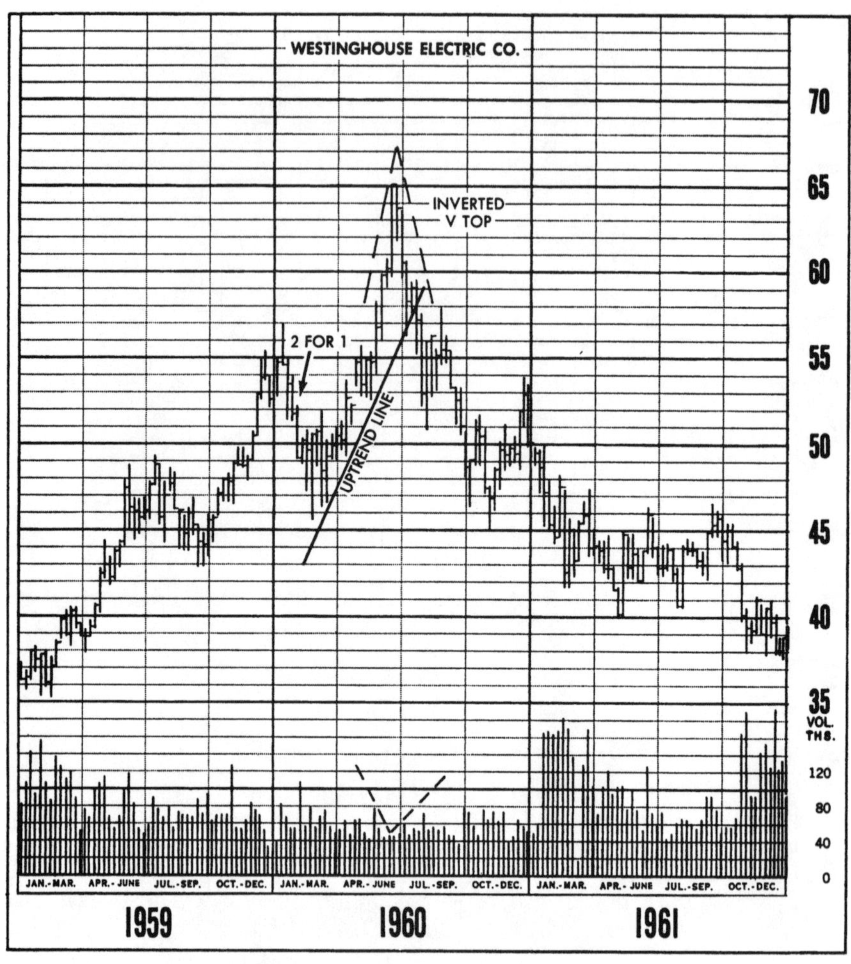

PLATE 31 WESTINGHOUSE ELECTRIC (Weekly) — Inverted True V

The inverted true V or, simply the "V top" that formed on the weekly range chart of Westinghouse in 1960 would have been extremely difficult to identify in the vicinity of the top. The only clues were (a.) the volume, which dropped very low at the apex, and then (b.) the breaking of major uptrend lines in July of 1960. However, the relatively sharp turn in January of 1960 might also have been mistaken for a V top. Although the other V turns illustrated on the preceding pages were much easier to anticipate, the chart analyst will be confronted with this tough one from time to time. Since this chart is a weekly range chart, analysis of a daily range chart probably would have helped to confirm a major reversal pattern not too far from the top. The daily range chart for the same period of time showed an entirely different pattern with similar forecasting implications. This happens in most instances, but chart trend indicators—daily or weekly—usually point the same way.

8

THE MEASURED MOVE

All price trends must come to a halt. Sometimes they switch into new directions without warning, as in V turns, but far more often they run into gradually increasing resistance. The pressure of buying comes to equal that of selling; as long as this rough balance continues, a stock moves horizontally across the chart. Market writers like to call this period of hesitation a "critical juncture," meaning the cat's on the fence and they don't know which way it's going to jump.

As the opposing pressures are building up or wearing down, their interplay in the market at this "critical juncture" may form one of the *reversal patterns,* meaning that a major switch in trend lies ahead. At other times, however, a stock is just pausing to digest a certain amount of support or resistance it has met, and once that's gone, it will resume its original trend. Such a pause, or hesitation, produces a *Continuation Pattern*—essentially, a more or less sideways trading range that interrupts, but does not end, a trend. Its chief value to chartists is in indicating future support areas and in forecasting the extent of subsequent price swings, as discussed in Chapters 2, 3 and 4.

That is nothing to sneeze at, but in a certain type of situation, we can do more—namely, to predict, from a price movement that has run into a hesitation area, *the probable extent of the subsequent price movement, or where the stock next will meet a "critical juncture."* We hereby dub this situation, which until now has been unnamed, the *Measured Move.* Such a move is, basically, a fairly large price swing that has been interrupted roughly at the midway mark, by either a fairly sharp "correction" (a rally or reaction, as the case may be), or by a horizontal congestion range. The interruption cuts the trend swing into two fairly equal legs, which tend to be parallel. In other words, the stock on each covers about the same price distance in about the same time (though sometimes the time is reduced on the second leg, which thereby becomes steeper than the first). Here's how it looks on the chart:

FIGURE 34

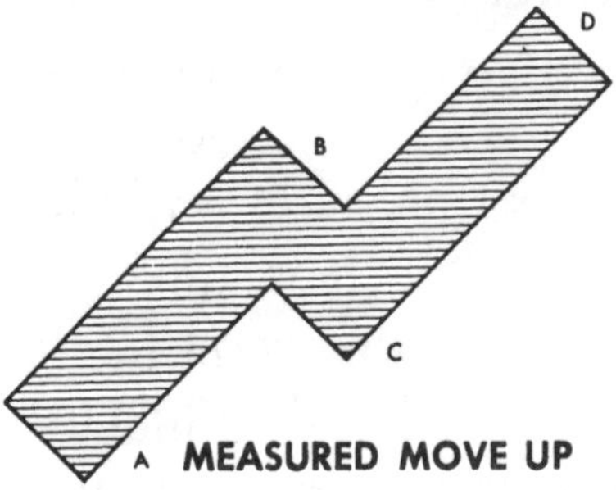

MEASURED MOVE UP

Note that the illustration is heavily shaded. This was done to avoid being distracted by the small countermovements contained within the broader waves. The same effect is achieved when one looks across a brokerage office at one of those big, framed wall charts of the market averages, covering many years. One then sees the major bull and bear markets, as mountain ranges and valleys, rather than the lesser moves. It is precisely such a broad picture on a smaller scale, of course, that one needs to analyze a Measured Move.

The components of a Measured Move, in detail, are:

A-B: *The first leg*. This may be either a long, gradual rise, or a fast, sharp run-up. The price will hold to a trend channel in a general way, but don't insist that a well-defined trend line be drawn along the lows of the move, for these trends often curve. Remember, look at the chart pattern broadly.

B-C: *The corrective phase*. This may be a sharp, quick reaction or a prolonged phase of consolidation. It is much like a railroad switch that shunts a train to a parallel set of tracks. The corrective action will mark the midpoint of the total rise.

C-D: *The second leg*. This move will very nearly equal that of the first leg. Note, however, that one should measure the indicated distance of the second leg beginning from the low point of the corrective phase (B-C). There is an important volume indication in this sector. Somewhere between the halfway mark and the two-thirds mark, on the second leg, volume tends to increase notably. Beyond the two-thirds mark, volume tends to drop off.

The Measured Move is just as valid in a decline as in a rise. The description above applies equally, in reverse.

Here is an example of a declining Measured Move:

FIGURE 35

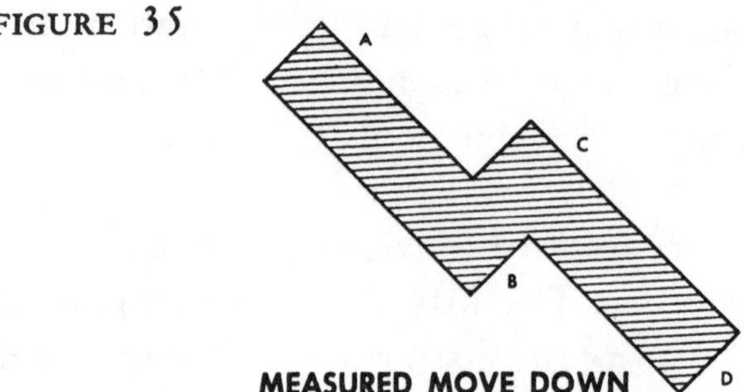

MEASURED MOVE DOWN

Now that we can recognize the pattern, it may be worth while to re-emphasize a point made earlier: there is no way of predicting a Measured Move before it begins. To try do so would be like trying to predict what kind of reversal pattern a stock will make at the end of a movement that is still in full progress. In either case, it is only after the pattern has been developing for some time that some determination of the possibilities can justifiably be made.

On the other hand, Measured Moves are easily readable in their late stages, and are extremely reliable indicators of the approach of a "critical juncture." They lend themselves remarkably well to the timing of market operations.

Why the Measured Move works as it does is not known, but we can speculate about it. It might be compared to a fast ball hurled over the plate, which a batter barely tips —just enough to give it a hop, but not enough to cut its momentum in the original direction. Slightly deflected, the ball flies on into the catcher's mitt—or, if he misses it, the ball sails on until it has lost the momentum the pitcher originally put into it. The corrective phase in a Measured

Move may be attributed to profit-taking, short selling, or any or all of the other motivations that may check a trend. Why the second leg is about equal to the first may take higher statistical mathematics or psychology to explain. Perhaps it's related to the fact that stocks tend to retrace half of the distance gained in any swing (the 50% rule). But regardless of the reason, there *is* a close correlation between the first and second legs of a Measured Move, which can be exploited by the chartist.

Let us now go over some actual case histories. If these analyses demonstrate that the reader can master the Measured Move, then by all means he should add it to his collection of valued tools.

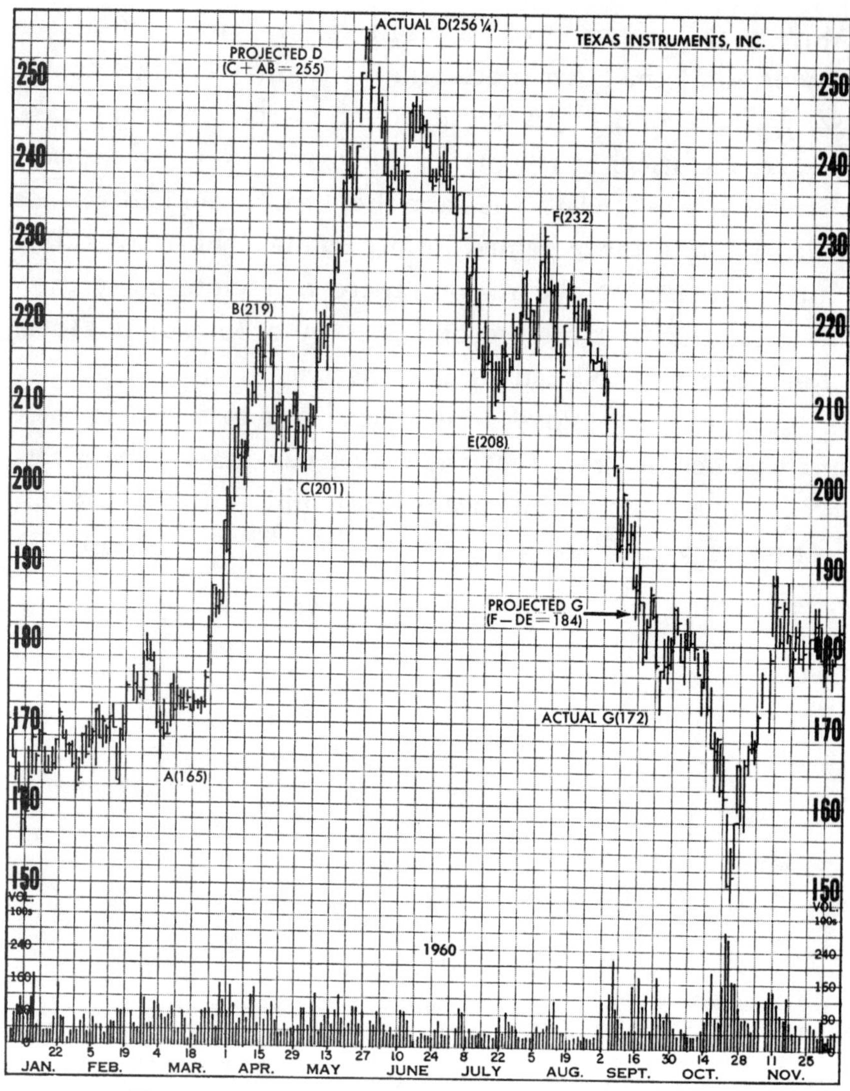

PLATE 32 TEXAS INSTRUMENTS — Measured Move

This Measured Move almost hit its objective on the nose. The move A to B (219—165 = 54) is expected to equal C to D. Adding 54 to C (201) projects the move to 255. The move reached 256¼ (D) or 1¼ points higher than expected. On the way down, D to E (256—208 = 48) should equal F to G. Subtracting 48 from F (232) gives a projected objective of 184. Actually, prices declined to G (172) and later spilled all the way to 149. Interestingly, the rebound from the low carried back to about the initially projected objective. Incidentally, Points B D F form a Head & Shoulders top.

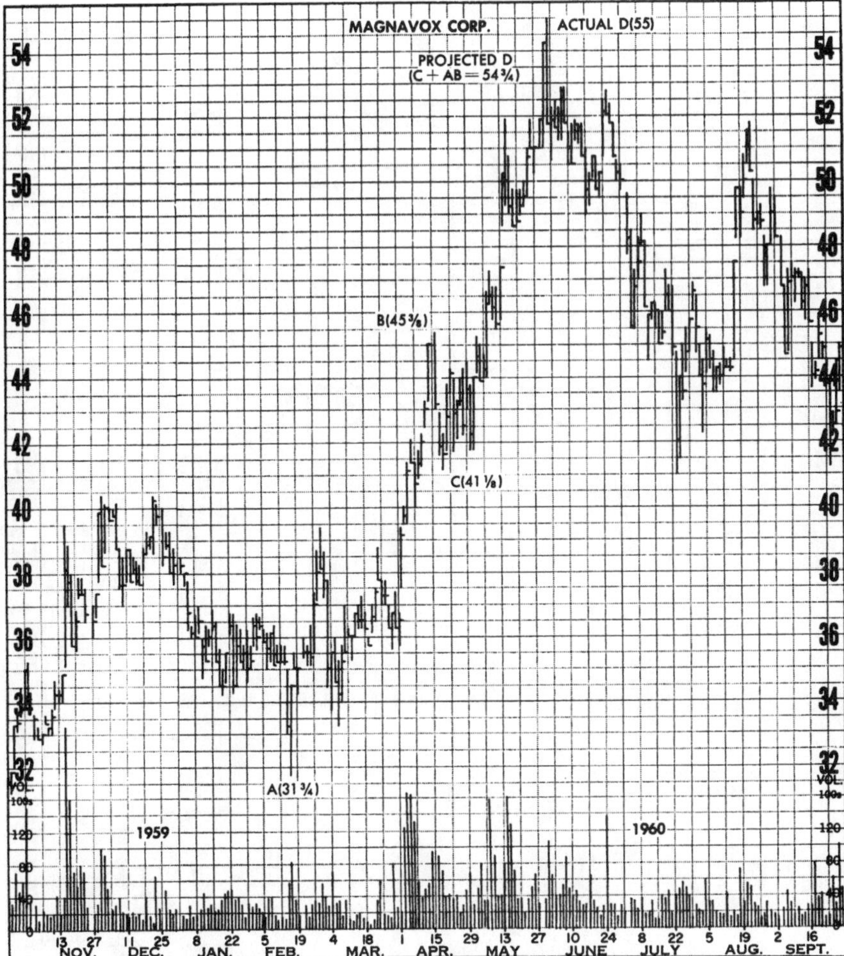

PLATE 33 MAGNAVOX — Measured Move

This chart was chosen to show how a Measured Move formation can be analyzed for a stock that does not particularly "chart well"—i.e., formations are not clearly outlined because of wide and jerky price swings and the prevalence of gaps. The bottom of the move in February (A) was 31¾ and the next substantial congestion area formed in April below 45⅜. The bottom of this congestion (C) is at 41⅛. To project the measured move to point D, subtract 31¾ (A) from 45⅜ (B) to get 13⅝. Add 13⅝ to 41⅛ (C) to arrive at the projected objective of 54¾ (D). Prices actually reached 55, exceeding the objective by ¼ point. A great majority of these formations do not come this close; they more often fall short of or exceed objectives by several points.

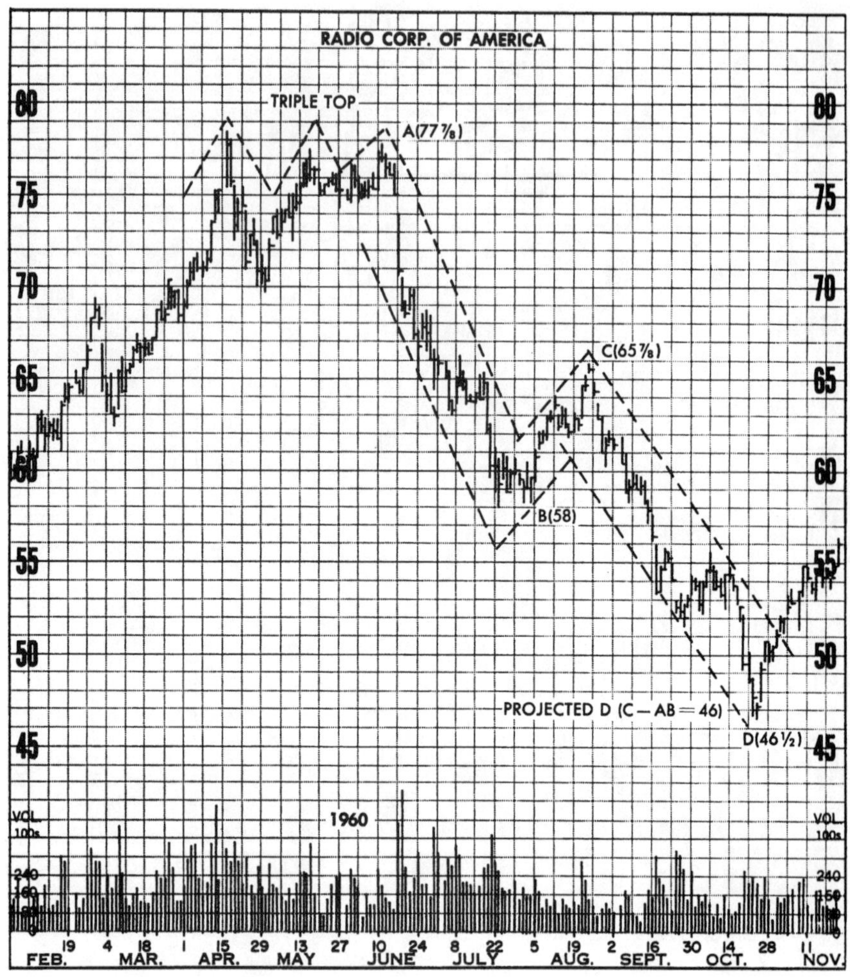

PLATE 34 RCA — Measured Move

This Measured Move, which marked a decline of 32 points for RCA in 1960, followed an interesting reversal formation. It might be called a Double Top with variations on the second top; however, the author would judge that the variations were sufficiently developed to cause the entire formation rightfully to be called a Triple Top. The decline of 19⅞ points from A to B was without a correction; there was a slight pause during the decline from C to D. By subtracting AB or 19⅞ from C, 65⅞, the decline can be projected down to 46. The bottom of the move, D proved to be 46½, just ½ point short of the Measured Move objective.

THE COIL (OR TRIANGLE)

When a stock fluctuates in progressively smaller price ranges, it is in effect winding up like a spring in a mechanical toy. And just as a wound spring holds enough tension to move the toy, a coiling action in a stock can propel prices. In the toy, the tension is mechanical. In the market, the tension builds on the increasing uncertainties of buyers and sellers. A typical coil (or triangle) looks like this:

FIGURE 36

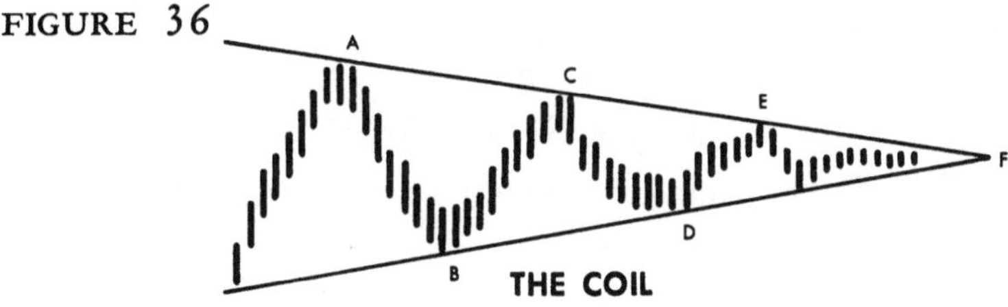

Invariably, a coil follows an advancing or declining phase of market action. In the example shown, prices are depicted as advancing to Point A, where evidently buying has dried up, and perhaps profit-taking develops. Here, a measure of uncertainty has been introduced in the minds of the "bulls." The reaction to B halts the profit-taking and attracts new buying. The ensuing rally to C upsets those who fear that prices are too high. The decline from C to D increases anxiety among the bulls, and the rally to E has the same effect on the "bears." Meanwhile, volume has steadily decreased through the coil as buyers and sellers alike become more uncertain about the future direction of prices. At the apex of the coil, Point F, buying and selling pressure for the moment reach complete balance. At this point, it takes very little new buying or selling to tip the balance and create a fairly sharp rally or decline. This accounts for the great difficulty of making a definitive price forecast from a coil.

WHICH WAY NOW?

More often than not—perhaps 60% of the time—this balance between supply and demand is only temporary, and represents nothing more than a pause in the long-range trend of prices. Therefore, coils are often regarded as indications of a continuation of the prevailing trend. But the other 40% of the time, coils become parts of other formations, or mark bonafide reversals. Even in such cases, the coil represents a balance between supply and demand, which has made the market sensitive to any new bullish or bearish influence. In some cases, the breakout itself, even though it was caused by small buying or selling, may be sufficient to swing a market sentiment that is evenly divided or uncertain.

While the word Coil suggests the *spring action* of this pattern, *Triangle* becomes more useful for further analysis. Now, the Triangle assumes one of four basic shapes on a stock chart: the Symmetrical (or Isosceles) Triangle, the

Ascending Triangle, the Descending Triangle, and the Inverted Triangle, or Funnel. They appear as follows:

Symmetrical Triangle: Lines drawn connecting the rally peaks and the reactionary lows tend to converge on the apex, or dead center, of the pattern. When the price breaks outside one of these lines —preferably on increased volume, the formation is regarded as completed.

Ascending Triangle: Here the top line, ideally, is horizontal, while the bottom line slants up to meet it. The picture suggests a "line of supply" available at the price represented by the top line, while demand becomes more aggressive—that is, more willing to meet the supply price—as time goes on. When demand finally overcomes the supply at that level, the price breaks above it, completing the formation. Volume remains relatively low during the formation, and should pick up on the breakout.

Descending Triangle: The opposite of the Ascending Triangle, it foreshadows a renewed decline. The lower line is a line of support, or demand. The supply, or offers to sell, become more aggressive with the passing of time. As sellers lower their ideas as to the value of the stock, the price works down until support gives way, the price breaks through the lower line, and the formation is completed. Again, volume tends to decline as the formation develops, and to pick up on the breakout.

Inverted Triangle: While this figure, which may also

be called a Funnel, looks like a normal Triangle turned backwards, it represents quite a different situation—a very nervous and uncertain market. In this case, volume *rises* as the price swings grow wider.

FIGURE 37

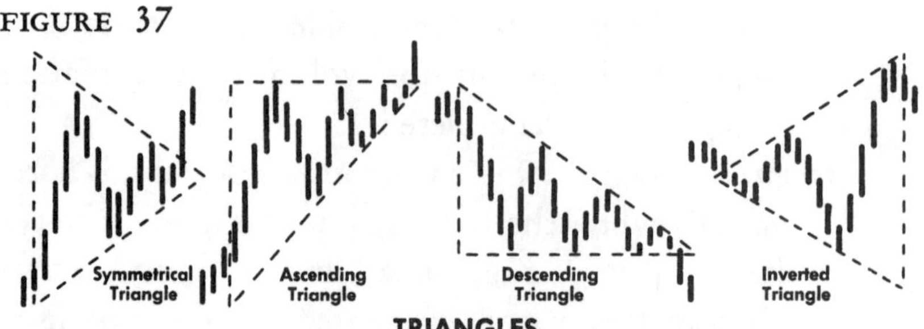

MARKET TACTICS

The analysis of Triangles should, of course, be tied in with other chart information such as trendlines, support and resistance, and other formations. The following guidelines are offered as a checklist in following Triangle developments:

1. Odds are favorable that any Triangle will eventually result in a continuation of the trend that preceded it.
2. The odds favoring a continuation decrease according to which of the four basic Triangles develops, in the following order: Ascending, Symmetrical, Descending, Inverted.
3. Purchases should be made at the lowest possible levels within a Triangle, or after the subsequent trend has been well defined, because Triangles are especially treacherous. They are subject to many false moves, and are among the least reliable of all chart formations.

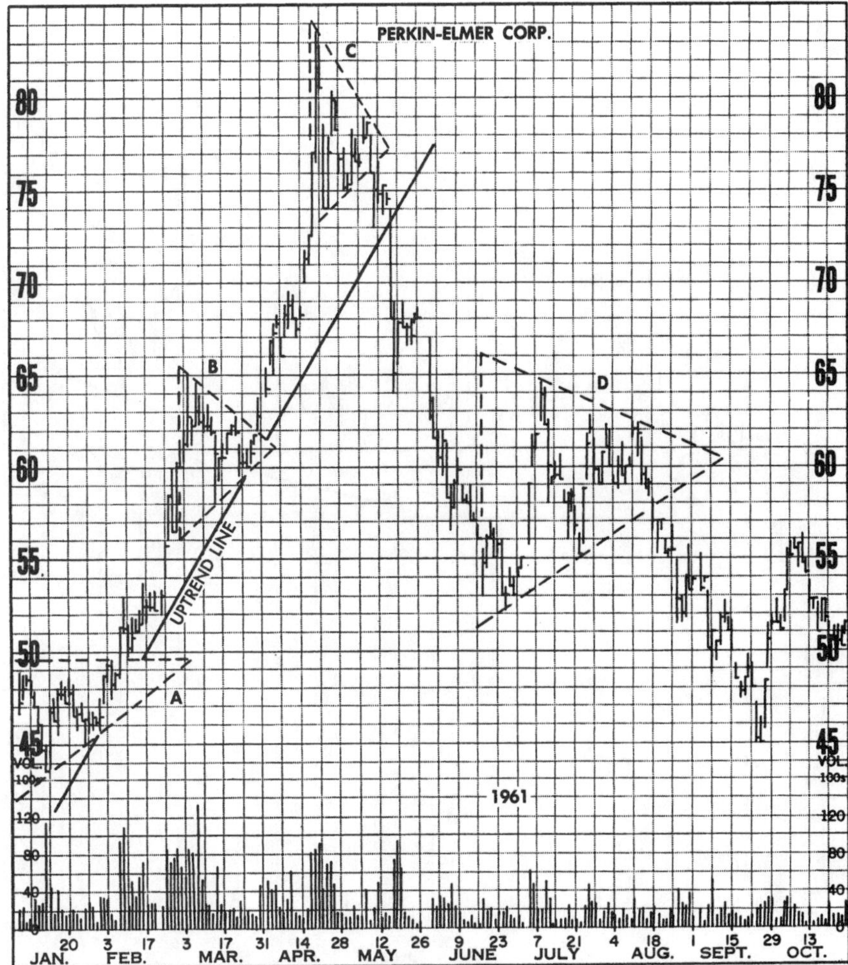

PLATE 35 PERKIN ELMER — Triangles

The chart of Perkin Elmer graphically portrays two of the four major triangles described in Chapter 9. The configurations are outlined and labeled A, B, C, D. Triangle A is an ascending type. It will be recalled that the first implication of a triangle formation is that it points to a continuation of the prevailing trend. Secondly, the ascending type favors a trend continuation more often than the other types. Triangles B and C are Symmetrical or Isosceles types of average size. In this case, B marked a continuation of the trend and proved to mark the midway point in the over-all advance. On the other hand, C evolved into a major reversal. Note how the initial breakout stopped at the uptrend line drawn along the Jan.-March lows. Soon, the trendline was broken on volume and a major downtrend was under way. Triangle D is a large symmetrical triangle, which proved to be a continuation pattern.

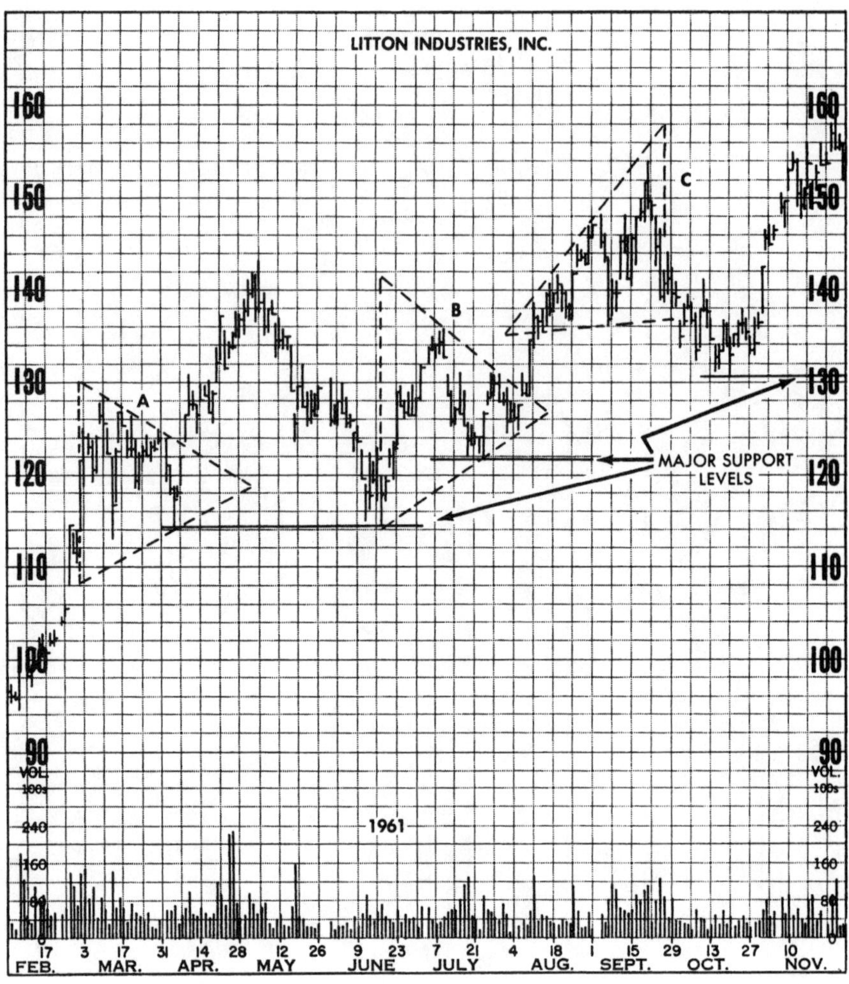

PLATE 36 LITTON — Large Triangles

The only significant chart formations that appeared during the 1961 bull move for Litton were relatively large Triangles (A, B and C). This cluster of Triangles, which could be confusing to the analyst while forming, nevertheless indicated a continuation of trend. (The stock started the year around 88 and reached 166 in December). A and B are almost perfect Symmetrical or Isosceles Triangles and C is an unusually well defined inverted triangle. The false downside breakout from C should not have been too disturbing to the chart technician, since this often occurs from this type of triangle. However, the inverted triangle signifies great uncertainty in the minds of buyers and sellers and, occurring at a high historical level, can warn of a top. In the above chart, major support levels were not violated. Incidentally, Triangles A and B taken together, began to look like the left and right shoulders of an incomplete large Head & Shoulders formation.

PLATE 37 STUDEBAKER-PACKARD — Triangle Top

Throughout 1959, 1960 and 1961, Studebaker was consistently among the five most active stocks on the New York Stock Exchange. On some days in 1959, it accounted for as much as 10 percent of the entire trading volume. This overall level of activity did not alter the significance of the chart formations. Coils and triangles predominated. A, which was a Descending Triangle, evolved into a major top. Prices returned to the apex of triangle A, and then formed a large Isosceles, or Symmetrical triangle, B. Triangles C and D are both descending types and correctly forecast the continuation of the decline. When the reader has finished the next chapter (10), a very pretty Pennant formation, which heralded the September-October advance, will come into focus.

10

CONTINUATION PATTERNS

Even the strongest trends do not roll on without interruption. They run into profit-taking, support or resistance levels, or other interference. Momentarily, the force behind the trend weakens, or the opposing side puts up a flurry of resistance. The interplay of supply and demand begins to draw a new pattern on the chart. If it signifies an important shift in the balance of power, we call it a *Reversal Pattern*. If it represents only a pause, after which the original price trend will resume, we call it a *Continuation Pattern*.

Technically, the Triangle is often placed in this class, because it most often is followed by a continuation of the previous trend. Too many times, however, the Triangle betrays its class and produces a Reversal. Hence, this tricky pattern rated a separate examination. Now let's examine a whole group of much more reliable Continuation Patterns: Boxes, Flags, Pennants, Wedges and Diamonds. Their graphic names describe them quite accurately.

FIGURE 38

Price fluctuations, over a period of weeks or months, outline a square or rectangle. These patterns are quite common; they usually represent a situation where a stock is caught between equally strong supply and resistance levels, and vacillates between them for a time, with neither buyers nor sellers able to assume the ascendancy. A breakout from a Box (unlike the Triangle) is usually valid and points the way for the ensuing price move.

FIGURE 39

The chartist's Flag must be pictured as flying without much of a breeze (otherwise it would assume the shape of a Box). Ideally, it forms a parallelogram slanting downward about 45 degrees. The flagpole is created by a sudden, sharp rise on good volume. The folds of the Flag—fluttering, if you will—are created by the subsequent fluctuation of the stock as it slips back. Loosely formed Flags, or broad Flag patterns, are not to be trusted, especially if they tilt upward, instead of sagging. But the tightly built

Flag, formed relatively quickly, is among the most trustworthy of chart formations—even if it tilts upward. Its reliability may be based on the fact that a simple, common pattern of market psychology can account for the Flag. A sharp run-up on good volume creates a flagpole. It also creates a good number of potential sellers, who would like to cash in on their profits, and the rise in prices may have exhausted much of the immediate demand. Hence, prices tend to drift down on decreased volume. Each successive low is lower than the preceding one, and each rally fails to top the previous rally high, because demand is temporarily weakened. This sagging tendency will halt when the new sellers have been satisfied. Now, prices resume their original course and, reassured, the buyers come out of hiding.

FIGURE 40

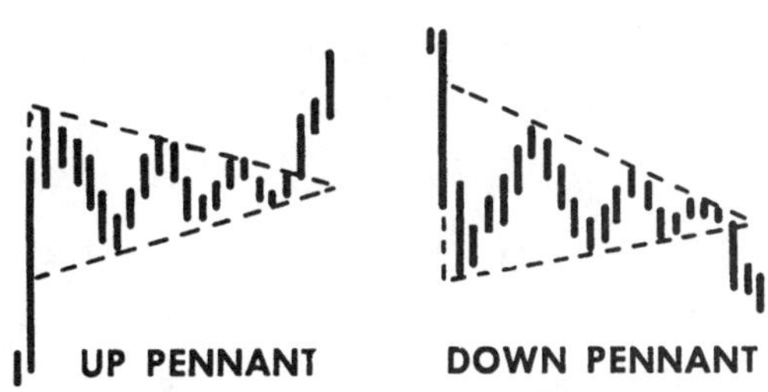

Like the Flag, the Pennant flies from a pole, created by a sharp rise on good volume. However, the Pennant has a stiff breeze behind it. Instead of sagging, like the Flag, it generally develops along a horizontal line, and takes a triangular shape. This implies a greater balance between supply and demand during this period of consolidation than in the case of the Flag. Volume patterns are about the same. Pennants are somewhat more reliable than Flags, and the tighter the Pennant, the more reliable it is as an indicator of a renewed, vigorous price trend.

FIGURE 41

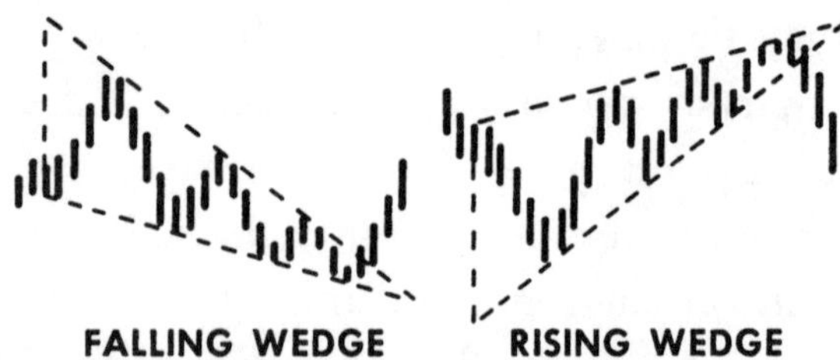

Wedges are a mixture of other patterns already discussed. They may resemble Flags, except that the lines formed by the tops and bottoms of price fluctuations tend to converge, rather than remain parallel. If a Wedge forms following a sharp price movement that can be designated as a "pole," it may look like a downslanting Pennant. Then again, it may embody some of the characteristics of a Triangle, but the Triangle is a horizontal figure, while the Wedge slants, either up or down. This slant—and only this slant—distinguishes the Wedge from other Continuation Patterns. Falling Wedges tend to focus within a major uptrend and are usually bullish and, strange as it seems, rising Wedges tend to occur in downtrends. Volume, as in most of the others, tends to dry up during the formation of a Wedge, and to pick up on the breakout.

FIGURE 42

The Diamond is most often found after a big swing in price. It is an exciting time, with the public alternately enthusiastic about the stock and worried about it. This naturally causes prices to fluctuate. If there were less excitement, prices would hold in a more or less horizontal channel, reflecting a momentary balance of supply and demand. Instead, prices seesaw with greater and greater swings, on high volume. Then the excitement begins to fade, the price swings contract and volume declines noticeably. The highs and lows of this period now form a Diamond. When prices later break through its high or low, volume may be expected to pick up sharply.

Diamonds are trickier than the other Continuation Patterns we have just discussed—in fact, some of them develop into Reversal Patterns. Further, they sometimes are confused with other types of patterns. The price movement may look like a Head and Shoulders, or an Extended V. The distinguishing marks of the Diamond are its upper and lower points, and its volume behavior. One pattern of development after Diamonds form is worth noting. Often, prices will break down through an apparent Diamond top and later turn to rally to sharply higher ground. Tricky or not, Diamonds often are followed by exciting developments; as every woman knows, they are worth collecting.

MARKET TACTICS

Breakouts from tight Boxes, tight Flags and tight Pennants are exceptionally reliable signs of future trends. They not only indicate the direction prices will move, but they also usually precede fast and wide movements. For this reason, some traders act *only* on such signals.

Not quite so reliable, but still among the more reliable of chart indicators, are loosely built Boxes, Flags and Pennants, and all Wedges and Diamonds. They can help to confirm other signs of a major trend development, and they of course are useful in locating levels of support and resistance and good buying or selling points.

CAUTION

It is always possible that an apparent Continuation Pattern may slip suddenly and without notice into a Reversal Formation. The chart follower must accept this risk as part of the odds, and remain alert and ready at all times to turn with the trend.

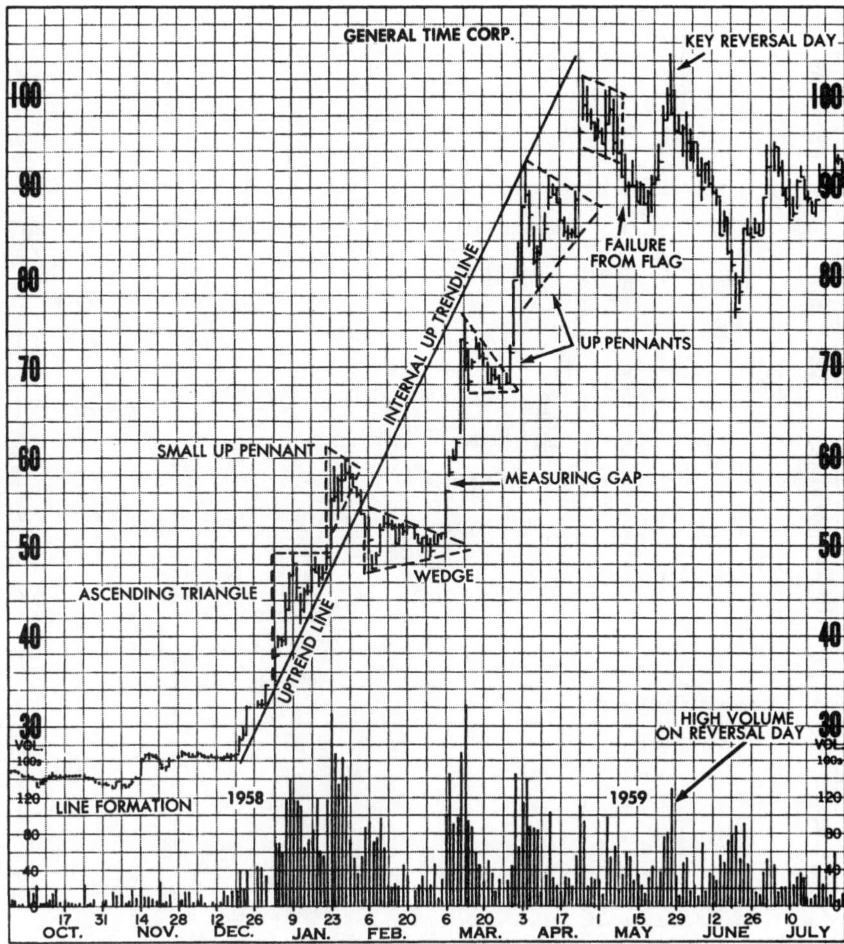

PLATE 38 GENERAL TIME — Key Reversal Day

This chart of General Time is a kaleidoscope of formations described in preceding chapters. Between September and December, a Line formation or Long Base prepared the way for a vigorous bull move. Triangles, Flags, Pennants and Gaps heralded the advance. A sharp uptrend line was penetrated on Feb. 5, but the advance resumed along the underside of the trendline extended. In Chapter 2, this was described as an Internal Trendline. Of interest are the Pennant (end of January) and the Flag (end of April) which were not completed. In both cases, new highs were made later, but the breakdown of the Flag did warn of an impending top. The Key Reversal Day was on high volume and marked the beginning of a decline that lasted five months and carried prices back to 60.

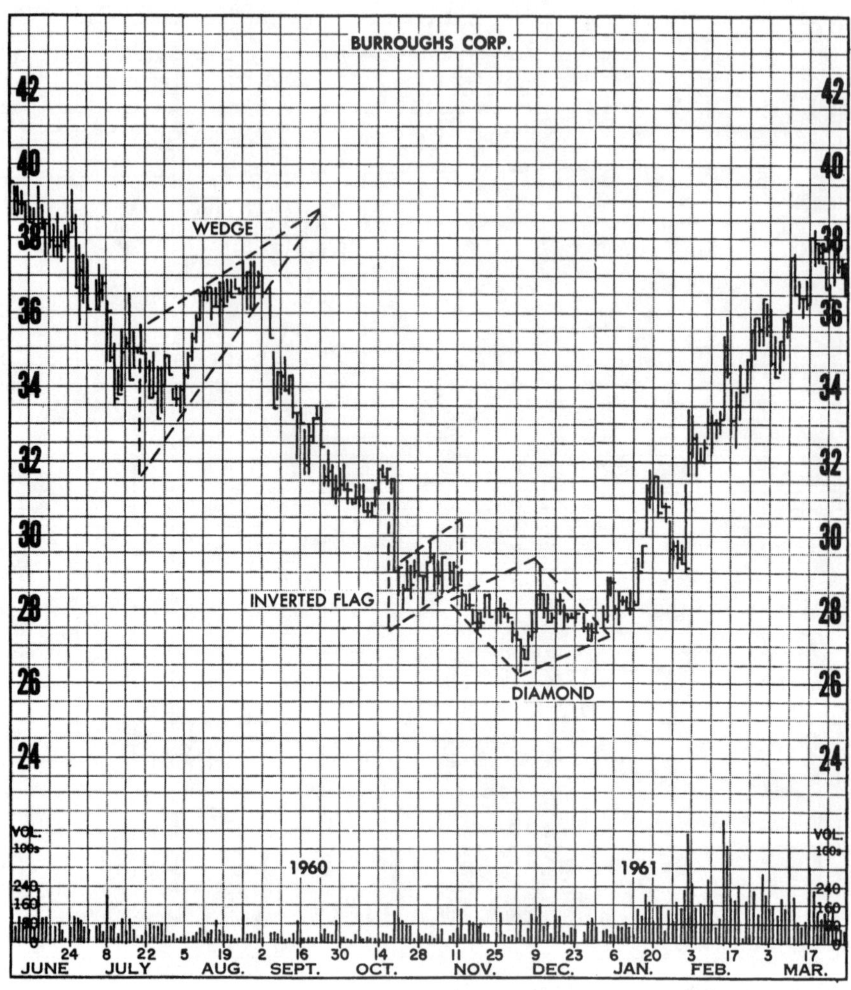

PLATE 39 BURROUGHS — Wedge, Flag, and Diamond

The first formation outlined left is a rather large rising Wedge. As explained in the preceding chapter, the tilt distinguishes the Wedge from a Triangle. Further, a rising Wedge has bearish implications, which is confirmed by a downside breakout. The Inverted Flag shows that flags form just as well upside down and are fairly reliable signs that a decline will continue, at least for the time being. Immediately after the Flag was completed, prices traced out a well-cut diamond, which here proved to mark a reversal in the major trend, an uncommon role for what is usually a continuation pattern—but a tricky one.

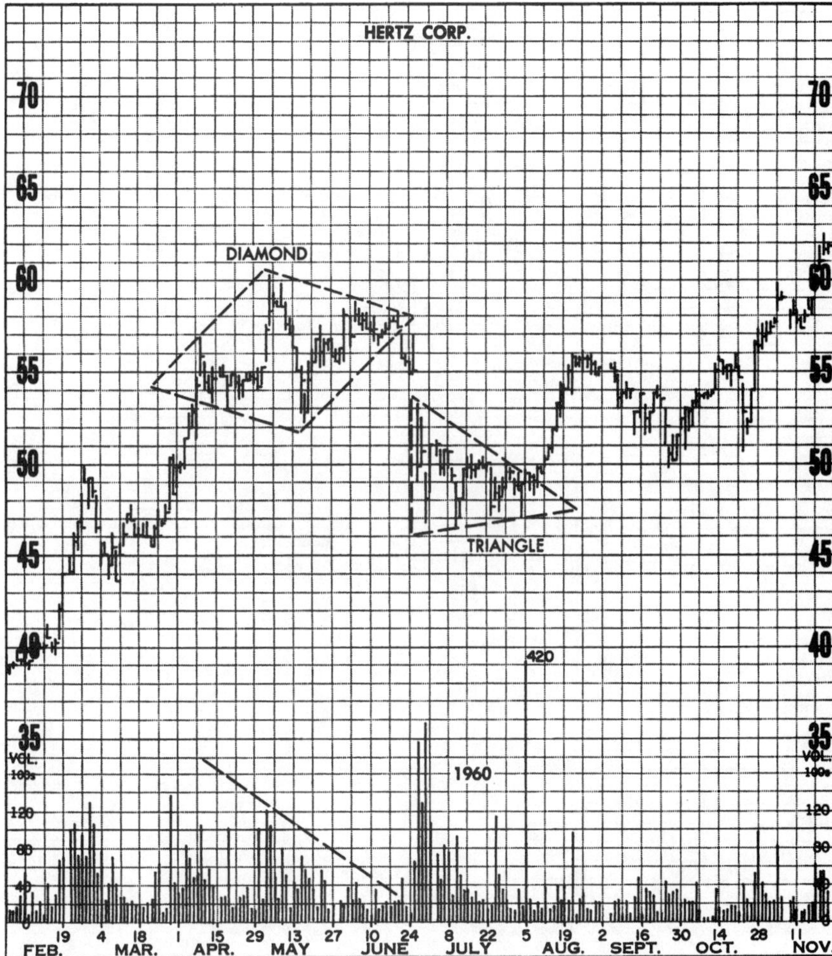

PLATE 40 HERTZ — Diamond

The Diamond outlined in April, May and June is of a type often mistaken by inexperienced chartists for a Head & Shoulders pattern. However, the difference can be easily distinguished by the experienced chart reader. In the first place the decline from the head carries below the low of the supposed left shoulder. It can be added that in most Diamond formations, it would be difficult to recognize shoulders. In this chapter, a behavior pattern was described which fits the illustration above. As stated on page 126, "Often, prices will break down through an apparent Diamond top and later turn to rally to sharply higher ground". Here the Diamond proved to be a continuation pattern, even though the initial breakout made it look like a reversal.

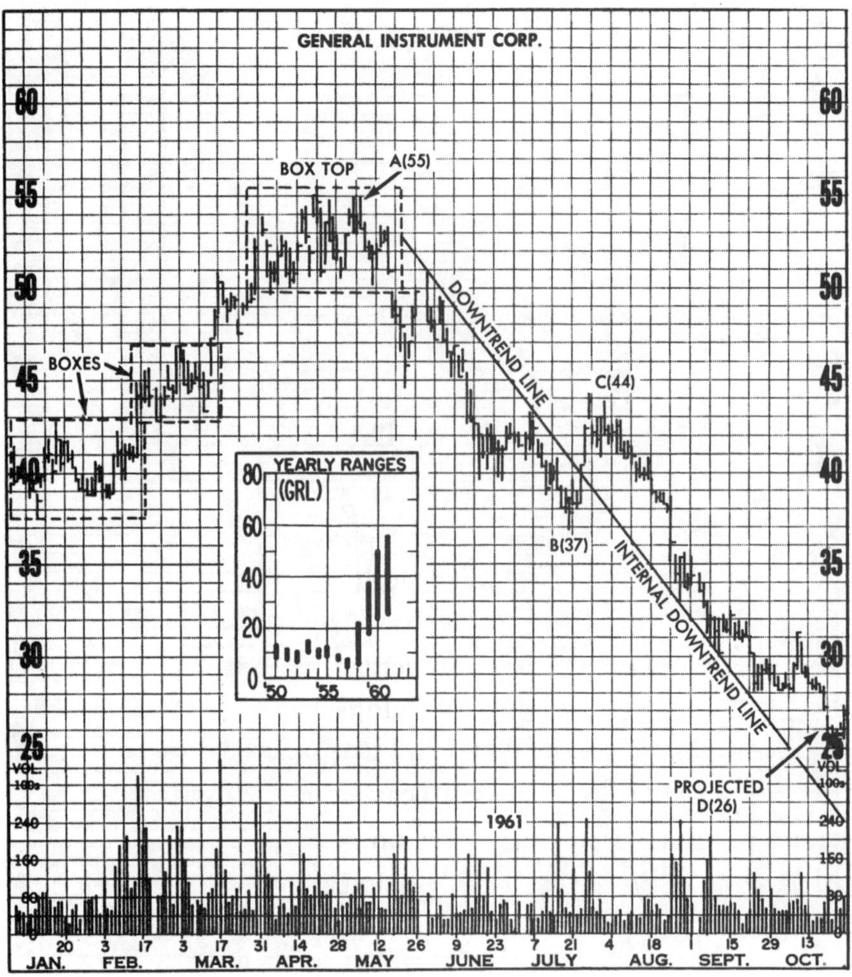

PLATE 41 GENERAL INSTRUMENT — Boxes and a Box Top

A series of Boxes featured the chart of General Instrument in early 1961. The third one evolved into a major top, which set the stage for a decline that wiped out about 55 percent of value in less than five months. As explained in the preceding chapter, Box formations are usually continuation patterns, and only infrequently signal major turns. The long-range chart picture can be helpful in finding these exceptions. At 50-55, General Instruments was selling at all-time highs after a four-year advance. Such heights should make anyone a bit queasy. Second, (not shown here), a Measured Move objective was achieved at 55. And third, a major trendline was broken on the completion of the pattern. The decline that ensued proved to be an excellent illustration of an internal trendline and a downside Measured Move formation. Note how prices, after breaking the initial downtrend in July, then adhered to the top side of the trendline, and how swing A to B almost exactly equals C to D.

REVERSAL DAYS, GAPS, ISLANDS

Over the years, chartists have built up a graphic language to describe interesting patterns. Among the terms that should be familiar to the diligent investor are four that designate sudden, striking developments. These are Key Reversal Days, High Activity Days, Gaps and Islands. Their reliability as trend forecasters is limited, but they do turn up rather frequently on one stock chart or another, and at times one of these events will mark a major shift in trend, at short notice. Hence, the appearance of any of these phenomena calls for close examination of the situation.

REVERSAL DAYS

A stock has been rising for some time. On this particular day, it pushes to a *new high* for the movement, then suddenly runs into heavy selling. The price drops sharply, and closes *below the close of the day before*—in other words, at a loss for the day. This combination of a new top and a loss for the day is called a *Top Reversal Day.*

Conversely, a *Bottom Reversal Day* occurs during a downtrend, when the price hits a *new low* for the move, then rallies to close with a *gain* for the day.

FIGURE 43

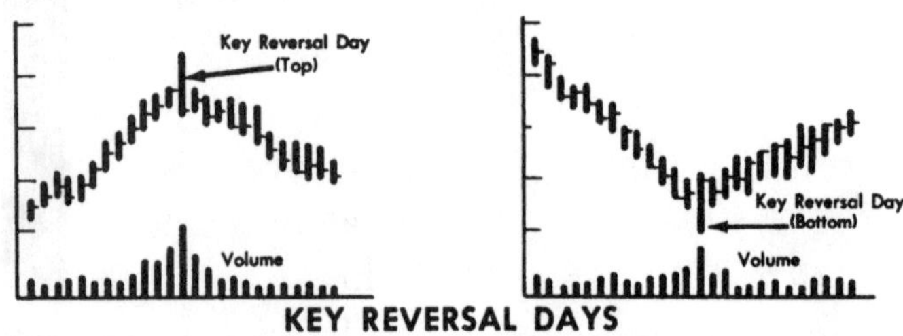

KEY REVERSAL DAYS

Generally, such Reversal Days mark no more than a brief interruption in the prevailing trend, or possibly a slowdown in the advance or decline, as the case may be. Much less often, a major shift in direction ensues. In such a case, the date is called a *Key Reversal Day*. It's easy enough to recognize—once the new trend is well established. Detecting it within a few days is harder. Unusual volume would be a clue. Others should be sought—for example, the chartist should try to determine whether the Reversal Day came at an important support or resistance level.

It may be that, after a long advance without a correction, some traders have become a bit nervous, and have decided to sell on the first sign of weakness. This comes when the stock hits a new high and then reacts to show a loss during the same day. The Reversal Day signal itself may cause enough stockholders to sell in the following days to set off a chain reaction.

The Key Reversal Day that occurs at the bottom of a major decline may be a bit easier to identify and explain. The last of the "bulls" have now lost hope, after having hung on for so long, and they decide to dump their stock and take their losses, in fear of worse to come. As they unload, and the price hits a new low, brokers may begin calling customers for more margin, resulting in still further selling. Prices drop sharply in frenzied trading. Then, as in a summer storm, the selling suddenly subsides. Short sellers buy a little stock to close out their positions and collect their profits. They and other buyers meet few offerings, and prices rise easily, closing above the preceding day's close. Traders note the selling climax and the day's gain, and decide to buy for at least a Return Move.

FIGURE 44

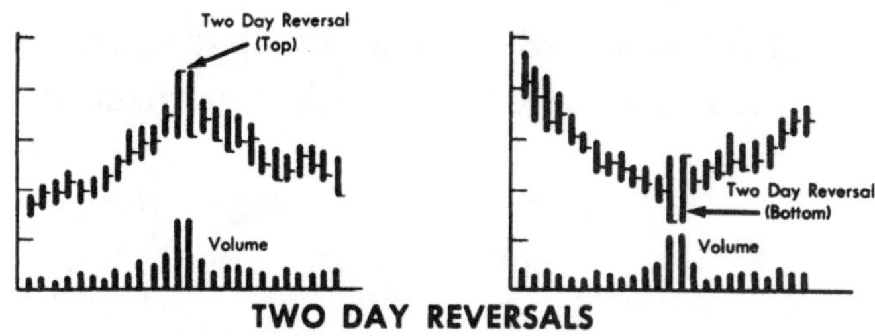

TWO DAY REVERSALS

A variation of the above formations is the *Two-Day Reversal*. Let's suppose that a stock has made a major advance. On the first day in question, it moves on to new highs and closes at about the high of the day. On the second day, prices may open about unchanged, but drift down and sell off toward the end, closing at the low of the day, which is also about the low of the preceding day. Presumably, after the bullish performance of the first day, traders expected the stock to maintain the advance. But their confidence is shaken when, instead of making a new high, the stock drops to yesterday's low. Such a shock may lead to a major reversal, if other conditions are ripe. Here again, high volume would be a helpful clue. And, as with the one-day reversals, the two-day variation may occur at the bottom of a decline, as well as at the top of a rise.

GAPS

Every now and then, a stock will open one morning at a price higher than the highest price of the day before, and keep rising. Or it will open lower than the lowest price of the day before, and keep falling. Either event will leave a conspicuous *Gap* on the chart—conspicuous because in the normal course of trading, the range of prices paid on any given day will overlap the ranges of the day before and the day after. A Gap *can* be informative to the analyst, but first he must determine what kind of Gap it is, and examine the chart characteristics of the stock that made it.

FIGURE 45

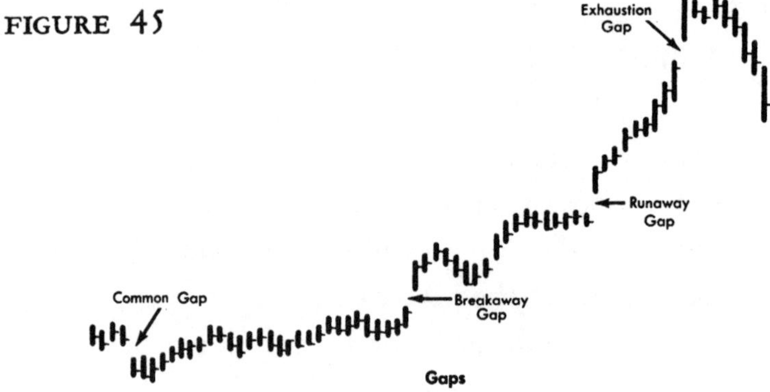

Gaps

The Common Gap: Active stocks relatively produce few Gaps, though those are the most significant ones. Gaps are much more often found on the charts of stocks traded very lightly, in which a single relatively small order to buy or sell may cause a wide swing in price. It would seem obvious that such Gaps are virtually meaningless. Nevertheless, oldtime chartists insisted on building a theory on this slender foundation. Usually, the price of a stock that has produced a Common Gap will fluctuate back past that area in a short time. This is called "filling the Gap." The old-timers held that *every* Gap must be filled—even if it took a lifetime. Traders would be well advised not to commit their funds on that assumption alone. As always, they should give careful attention to the past pattern of prices and volume before judging the significance of the Gap.

The Breakaway Gap is a horse of a different color. It generally occurs after an important chart pattern has been completed, and it often marks the beginning of a major price move. An *upward* Breakaway Gap is usually accompanied by a big rise in volume, and is likely to show a greater than normal range between the day's high and low prices—in other words, a longer vertical line on the chart. A *downward* Breakaway Gap *may* be accompanied by heavy volume, but volume is not quite so important here. Up or down, the breakaway represents some overnight development that has caused a concentration of orders to buy (or sell) at the market price. The development often is an unexpected news event—a stock split, dividend action, a merger, Government action, a war scare—of sufficient importance to shift market psychology for a considerable time, resulting in a major price movement. Such Gaps are sometimes "filled" by an early reaction in prices, but more often the stock accelerates its movement in the direction of the breakout. In the days following the initial Breakaway Gap, it is not uncommon for a stock to produce one or more additional Gaps, as excitement about the situation spreads.

The Runaway (or Measuring) Gap: Sophisticated traders prefer to buy on reactions, and often wait for one after a major advance has got underway. Sometimes, however, the stock, instead of reacting, *accelerates* its advance. Then the waiting traders may jump aboard, in fear of missing the bus altogether. At the same time, those who have sold short may see a big rise ahead and hasten to buy, to reduce their losses. And the move may stir excitement in the general public. A new wave of buying develops from these sources, creating a series of aptly named Runaway Gaps. These are also called Measuring Gaps, because they often occur at about the midpoint of a major price swing, and hence can be used to measure the likely extent of the move. For example, if a stock formed a base in the $20 to $22 area, then climbed to $40, where a Runaway Gap formed, there is a fair likelihood that it will go on to the area of $58 to $60.

Exhaustion Gaps: As a long advance rolls on, more and more stockholders grow nervous as well as pleased. They rightly feel that this can't go on forever—but they'd hate to sell out and miss a good part of the rise. Now and then, venturesome traders will decide the stock is overpriced and will sell short, but as the rise gains momentum they rush to cover, feeding the buying boom. A final spasm of buying causes the price to form a gap or series of gaps. Now this may carry the stock into the area where a good many holders had long ago decided to take their profits. The rise may bog down in heavy trading, and the stock may "fill the gap" within a week or so. It would then be clearly an Exhaustion Gap, marking the final flush of buying, after which the "tired" advance will pause to rest, or yield to a downturn. A careful study of the whole situation is necessary to make an early distinction—a vital one

—between the Runaway and the Exhaustion Gap. (Both kinds, of course, occur in declines as well as rises.)

The Island Reversal: When an Exhaustion Gap is followed by a Breakaway Gap, as the stock trend turns sharply into reverse, the picture on the chart is graphically called an Island. For example, stock XYZ has been having a strong run-up. It reaches a climax one day—a Wednesday, let's say—opening at a new high in heavy volume and rising further, but demand begins to peter out, and fairly heavy profit-taking develops. The stock nevertheless closes with enough gain to leave a gap on the chart. Overnight, however, the selling orders build up so heavily as to cause XYZ to open below Wednesday's lowest price, and to keep falling. On the chart, the line representing Wednesday's trading range stands alone, cut off on both sides. This is called a *One-Day Island Reversal.* Other islands take two or more days to form. In either case, they signify at least a temporary halt in the prevailing trend, and may—especially when accompanied by unusual volume—indicate a major reversal in trend. (See the case study of Avnet at the end of the chapter.)

HIGH ACTIVITY DAYS

Any day when volume is exceptionally high or prices make an exceptional swing (often these go together) should be tagged by the chartist as a High Activity Day. It is apparent that some significant change in ownership occurred on that day, and at that price. Subsequent price movements will determine whether the buyers made a wise decision or a poor one. In any case, closer study may yield useful information. It may be, for example, that a big block of stock that has been available for sale at that price—in other words, "overhanging the market"—has been cleared away, leaving the stock free to advance against little selling pressure.

MARKET TACTICS

All the unusual phenomena discussed in this chapter—One- and Two-Day Reversals, Gaps, Islands and High Activity Days—should be regarded by the investor-analyst as *caution flags*. He must of course consider each case within the framework of the over-all chart picture, which includes trendlines, support and resistance levels and, possibly, reversal patterns. The special circumstances of each situation will determine whether one should buy or sell. It's not possible to outline a hard-and-fast rule, but on the other hand, one should not ignore a warning. Some of the case histories that follow show just how significant such warnings can be.

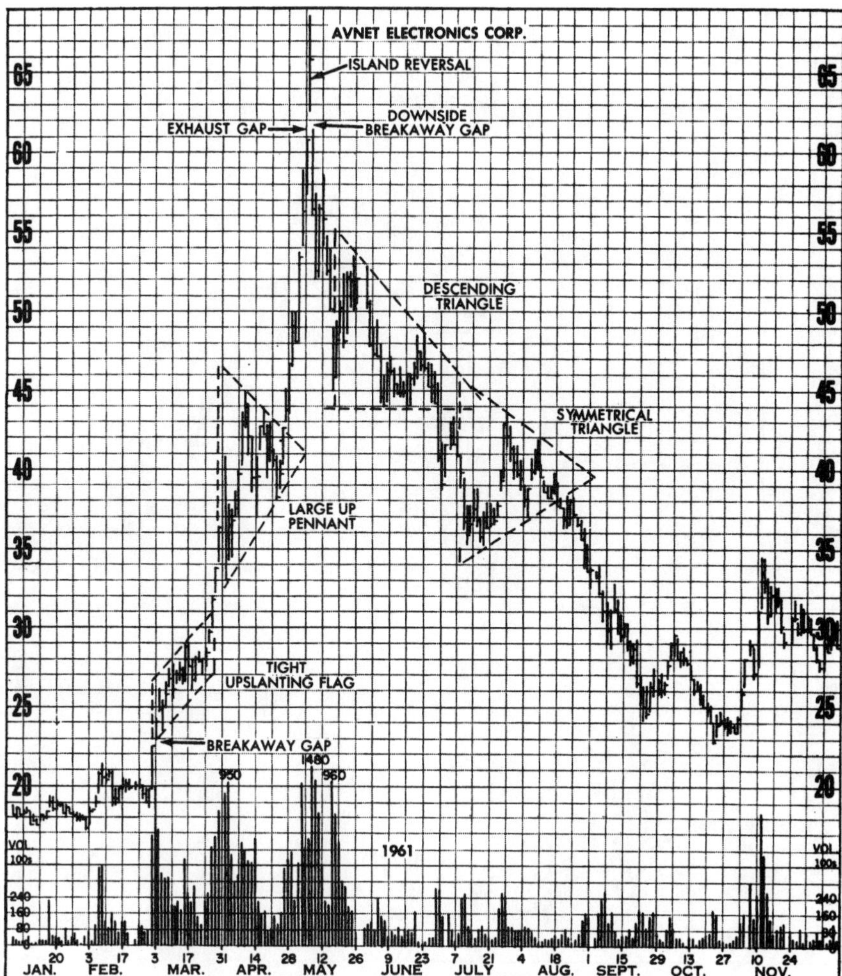

PLATE 42 AVNET — Island Reversal

The importance of studying a daily high, low and close chart is clearly outlined in this picture. In the very short period of less than 10 weeks, prices of Avnet exactly quadrupled (17⅛ to 68½.) Three days' action then outlined a classic major Island Reversal Top. This paved the way for a decline which just stopped short of giving back the entire advance. The island formed on May 8, 1961, when prices at the opening leaped ("gapped") to new highs and, on the following day, "gapped" back down and closed under the low of two days before. Volume, which was frenzied throughout the advance, reached a peak in the five-day period marking the top. All pertinent formations are outlined and labeled. As would be expected, the most "bullish" of formations, the tight upward-pointing flag and a large pennant, sparked the advance. Triangles featured the way back.

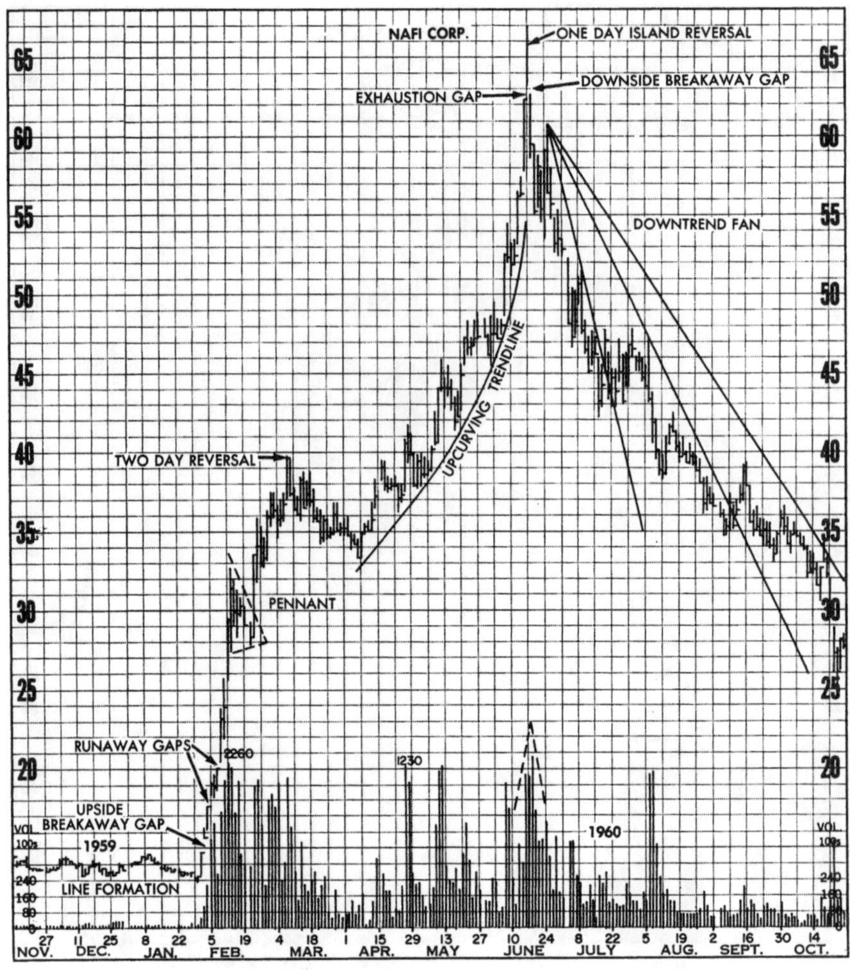

PLATE 43 NAFI — Gaps, Reversals, Islands

This is another chart that illustrates many of the formations analyzed throughout this book. First is the Line formation, the launching pad for the rocket-like price move. A Breakaway Gap and several Runaway Gaps left no doubt to the experienced chartist that prices were headed higher in no uncertain terms. Prices of NAFI doubled in six weeks and then ran into a Two-Day Reversal. In most instances, such an action completely reverses a trend, but for NAFI there was only a four week pause while the second stage of the price rocket ignited. A sharply curving uptrend led the way to the climax stage. Prices soared on a frenzy of volume, gapped to a new high (Exhaust Gap) and then gapped back down to complete an Island Reversal. The major decline developed as a fan, with the break of the third downtrend line later proving to be the end of the decline.

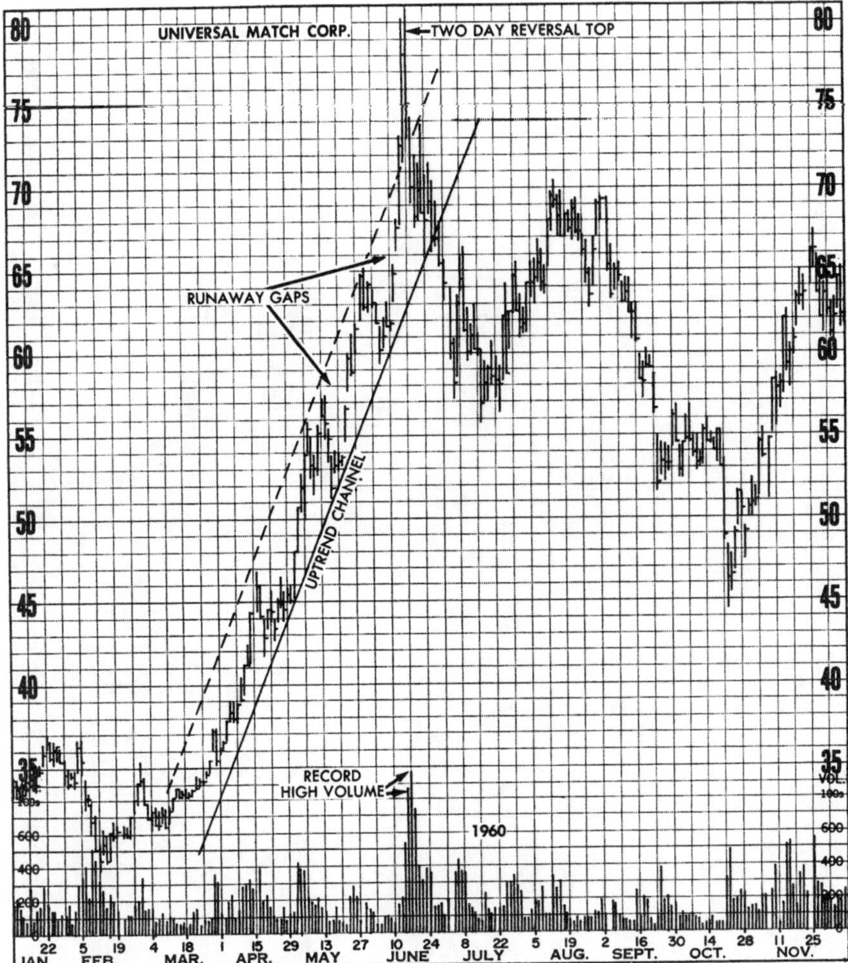

PLATE 44 UNIVERSAL MATCH — Two-Day Reversal Top

This chart was adjusted for a 2-for-1 split on June 15, 1960. Actually, the advance from below 29 in February to 80¾ in June represented a 112-point advance (before split) in just 18 weeks. As in many major advances, this one religiously followed a sharp uptrend channel and then climaxed (a vertical rise on exceptionally high volume.) On June 14, prices rose to new highs on the highest volume of the year to that date and closed near the high. On June 15, the high was barely exceeded, and prices closed not far from the low of the previous day. Volume again hit a new high. These two days proved to be the absolute top for UM for months to come. Chart buffs may argue that this top could more correctly be labeled a Key Reversal Day because June 15 marked a new high. They may be right. Whether this was a Two-Day or a one-day reversal, it was a humdinger. By February, 1962, prices were below $25.

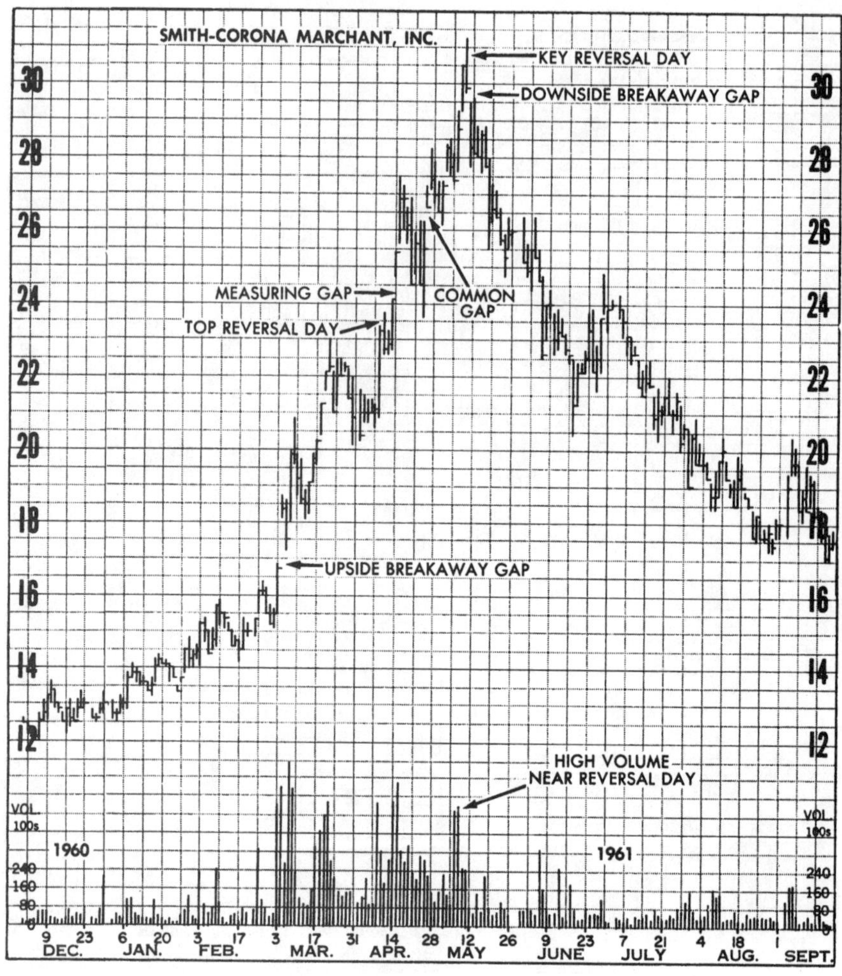

PLATE 45 SMITH CORONA — Key Reversal Day Top

The high of a major advance and the starting point of a major decline for Smith Corona in 1961 were signaled by a Key Reversal Day. Just one day's price action appeared to be sufficient to completely reverse a trend of several months' duration. Helping to confirm the one day's action as a top was a burst of volume on the two preceding days. The occurrence of the highest volume just before the reversal is common to this type of chart signal. Another important confirmation of the top was the downside Breakaway Gap after the reversal—also a common occurrence with one day tops. (See Avnet and NAFI chart) Other chart signals labeled are the Top Reversal Day, the Upside Breakaway Gap, The Runaway Gap and the Common Gap. The Top Reversal Day proved insignificant, as the advance was quickly resumed. The gap into new highs distinguished the Measuring Gap from the Common Gap.

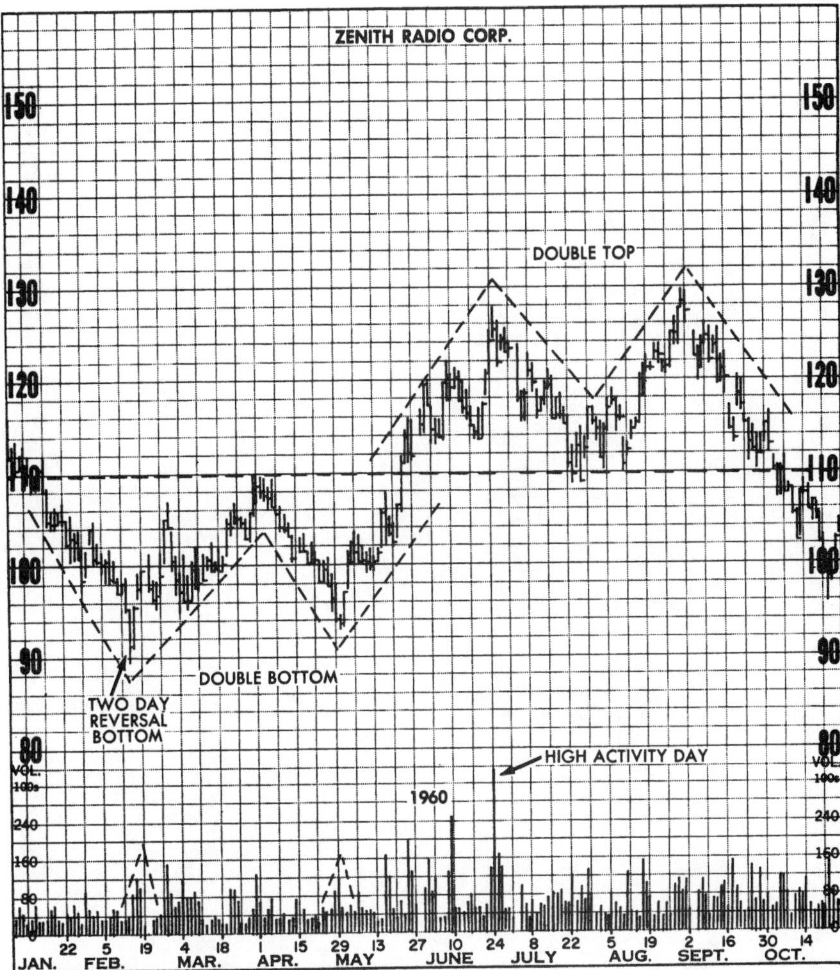

PLATE 46 ZENITH — Two-Day Reversal Bottom

In February, a Two Day Reversal halted a sharp decline and supported a fair recovery type rally. The two day bottom was challenged in May and again in October, but each time, prices failed to break through. This low held through early 1961 and proved to be the turning point of a move that carried almost to 250. Close examination of the Two Day Reversal Bottom will reveal that the price and volume range on each of the two days was wider than average. Another unusual chart "point of interest" was the High Activity Day on June 24, which pinpointed a heavy supply level and could have helped to anticipate the September 2 top. And finally, the overall chart pattern is unusual for its symmetry. A large Double Bottom (formed by the Two Day Reversal and the May reaction low) was almost exactly balanced by a large Double Top. The two bottoms and the two tops were approximately 10 weeks apart and the breakout level for both formations was the same (about 110).

THE TRAP

And now, as the fox might say to his cubs, it is time to talk about an unpleasant subject. Actually, the Trap is not so much a chart *pattern* as a *predicament*. It may be found as part of any number of patterns described in preceding chapters, or it may stand alone.

The analysts, with their flair for graphic terms, tag these situations as "*Bull Traps*" or "*Bear Traps,*" depending on which kind of trader they catch. Basically, a Bull Trap occurs after a stock has traded for a while in a relatively narrow range near recent highs. Prices break out of the range into new high ground and then suddenly decline through the lows (support levels) of the previous trading range, leaving the "bulls" (or rather those who bought the stock on its last rise or in the trading area), stranded with losses. The more significant Traps feature a splurge of volume; the more volume in the Trap, the more bulls have been caught. The Bear Trap is much less common. It occurs when a stock drops to a new low area on active trading from a congestion or trading range and then rallies back over the trading area. In most cases, a Trap is followed by at least an intermediate swing in price (10 to 25%) and often a major move (25 to 50%).

FIGURE 46

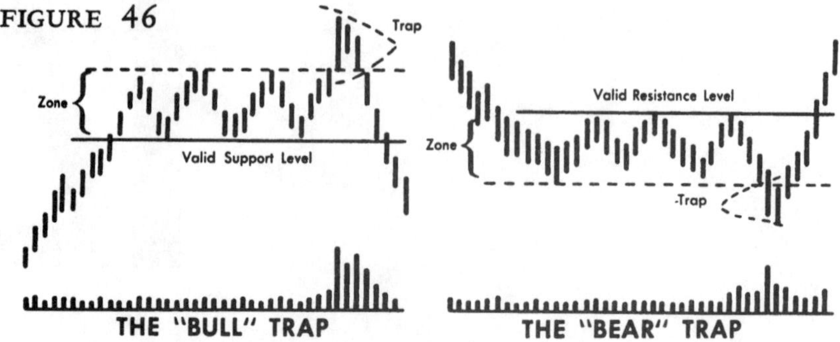

THE "BULL" TRAP THE "BEAR" TRAP

The stock in such a situation may be likened to a swimmer who, after standing by a pool for some time, finally dips his toe into the water—that is, the new high or low area—but finds it too cold and pulls out. In terms of market psychology, we may assume that a stock's penetration into new high ground has encouraged old buyers and has excited new ones—but it also has brought into play a large, heretofore invisible supply of stock available for sale at the new high price. The supply proves too great for the demand and the price declines. Confidence in the stock is disturbed, at least for the time being. The new buyers find themselves trapped with losses. Some of them accept the realities of the situation and sell out, thus adding to the pressure on the price.

The two keys to identifying such a situation are *unusual* volume and the backslide from a new high that *breaks through a previous trendline or support level.* Now, it is not a Trap formation at all, when a stock in a major uptrend hits a new high in active trading and then reacts on lower volume. In fact, that's perfectly normal behavior, and may be interpreted as bullish—so long as the reaction does not "violate" the indicated support level or trendline. (It is well to keep in mind at all times that in actual trading, there are as many shares *sold* as *bought*. If a stock can't make much headway on high volume, obviously, heavy selling pressure exists at this price level.)

MARKET TACTICS

The Trap is well named. It may catch even the most experienced chartist, because its beginning—a stock's hitting a new high or low—looks like a go-ahead signal. In most cases, that's just what it is. As we have noted, a stock moving in a given direction will tend to continue in that direction, and a breakout to a new high or low (especially after a congestion of price movements) offers strong confirmation that the trend will continue. Nevertheless, a sudden reversal, or Trap, is always possible—just as any chart formation may be reversed. Hence, the readiness to abandon a position as soon as it appears to have proven wrong is one of the most important attributes of the successful investor.

When a Trap develops after a long price movement, and is accompanied by high volume, a major trend reversal is indicated. On hitting a Bull Trap, holders should cash in their profits, and traders may sell short. In *any* Trap situation, the short-term trader who has been caught should take his medicine as quickly as possible and stay out of the situation until it has been clarified. The long-range investor should take a hard look at his position. If other factors—such as long-range chart considerations, the company outlook, his tax situation and the business cycle—are favorable, he may stay in and "sweat it out."

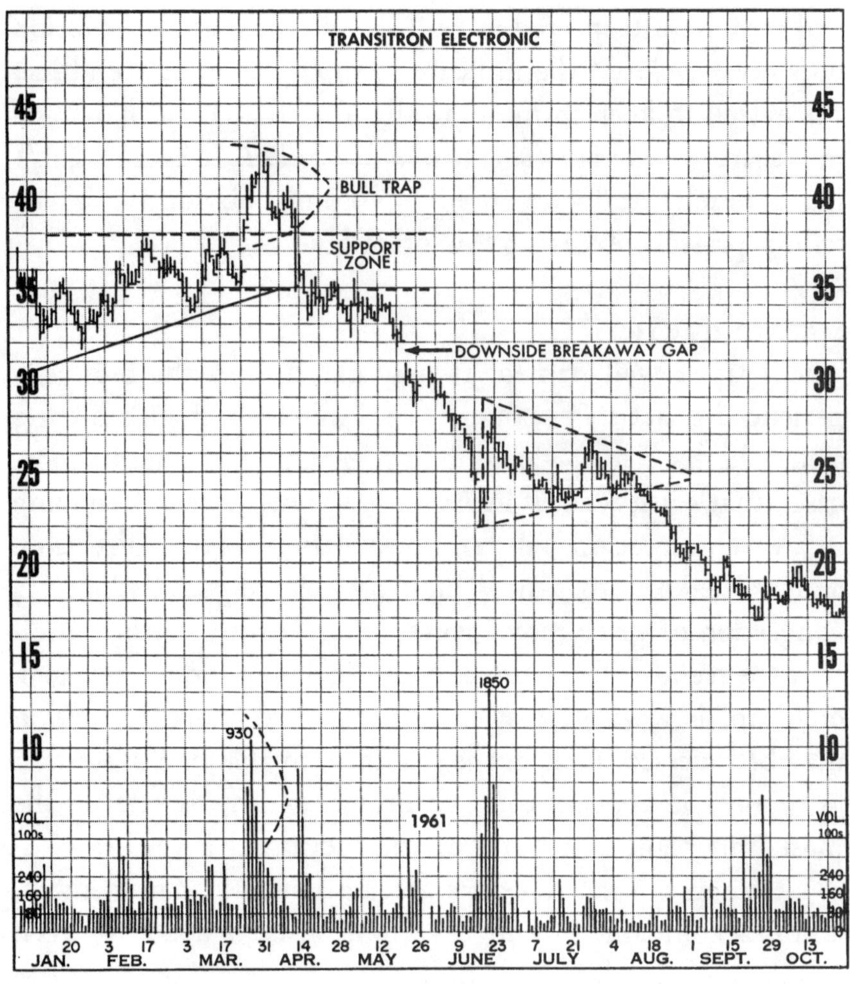

PLATE 47 TRANSITRON — The Bull Trap

This was a mean April Fool's Day joke on the bulls. (Well, April 1 was a Saturday, but the high was made on the next trading day, April 3.) The breakout to new highs was on very active trading, and volume remained high throughout the "trap" development. That meant that plenty of "bulls" were caught, and it set the stage for the subsequent decline (to 14⅛ by the end of Jan. 1962). At the time of the trap, prices had been leveling off for over six months after previously declining from 60. A chartist looking at the picture from Jan. 1, 1960, (not shown here) would conclude that the base was big enough to support a move back to the high (60). He would have also seen a potent resistance level at 45. At any rate, assuming he was caught in "the trap", the high volume on the reaction into the support zone on April 13 should have waved a red flag. And of course, any chartist would have known that the gap on May 17 into new low ground locked the gate for a long time to come.

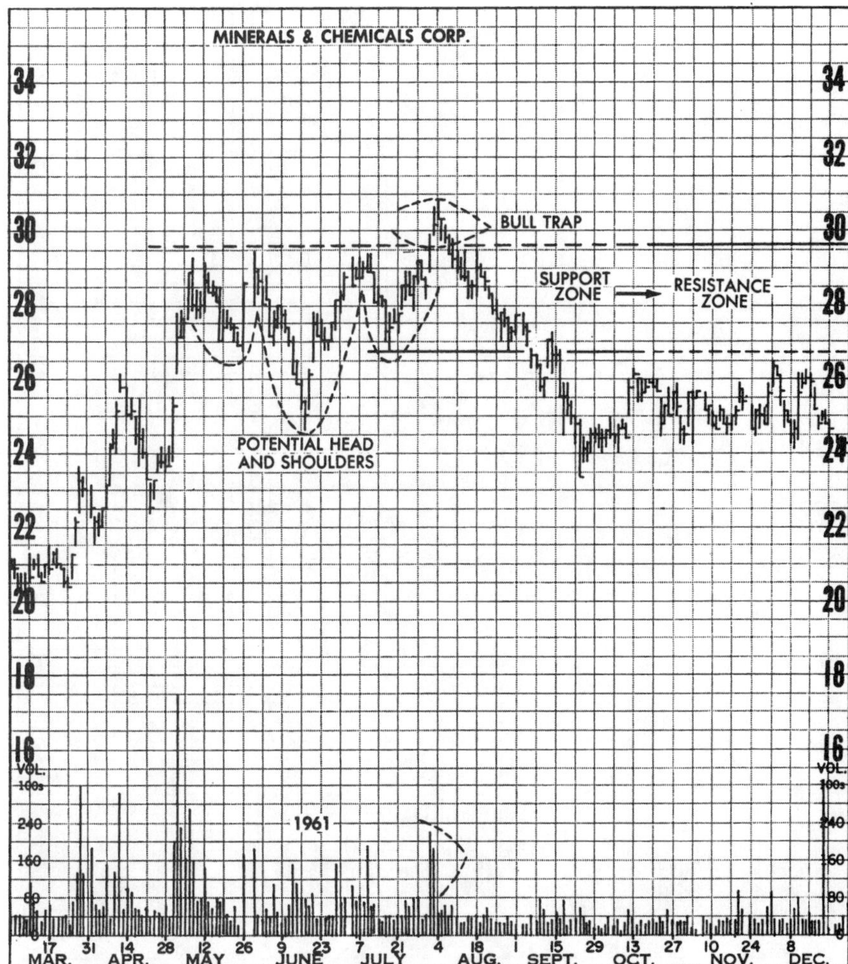

PLATE 48 MINERALS & CHEMICALS — The Bull Trap

This was a most unusual chart situation. In March, 1961, prices rallied from 20 to nearly 30. The chart then proceeded to outline what looked like an ideal Head & Shoulders bottom. After three unsuccessful attempts to clear the 29½ barrier, prices in early August finally broke through on volume to new highs, which would ordinarily signal a new vigorous advance. But lo and behold, prices reacted right through 29½—which should have been a support level after the breakthrough. The decline kept right on through the potential right shoulder, thus completing the trap of the "bulls" and setting up a further decline. "Monday morning quarterbacking" would point out that any Head & Shoulders bottom pattern that forms after an advance should be suspect. This has some validity, but there have been many perfectly valid Head & Shoulders bottoms at such an advanced stage. This simply was a rare example of a Head & Shoulders bottom that failed and ended up as an infamous bull trap.

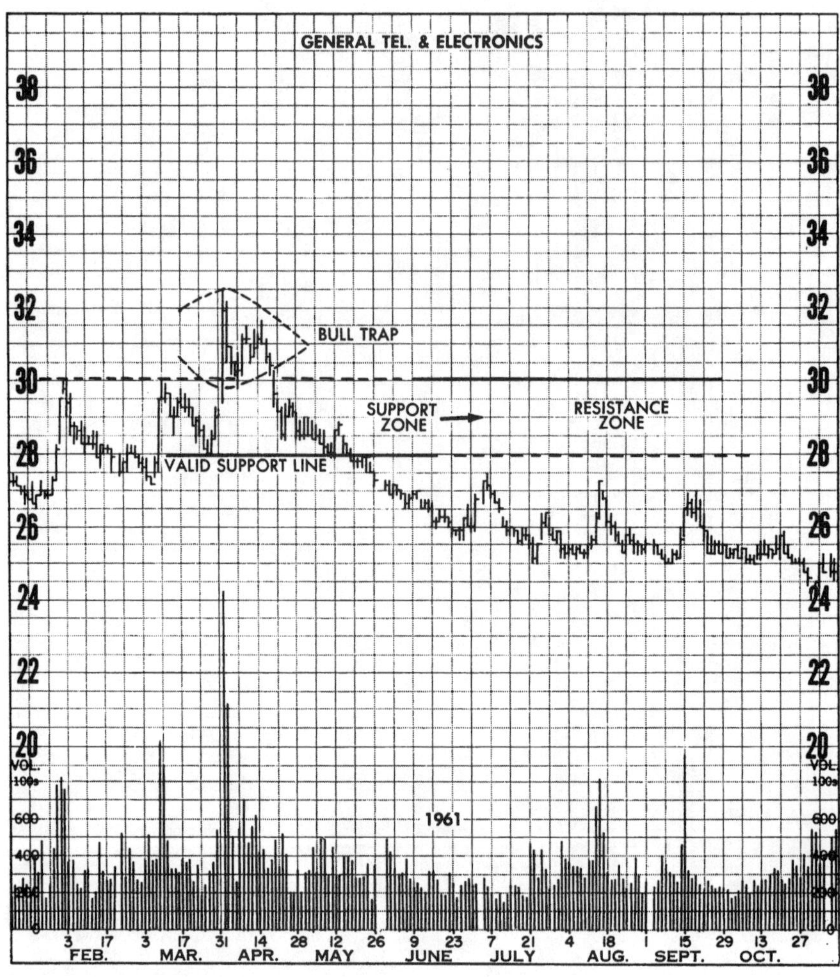

PLATE 49 GENERAL TELEPHONE — The Bull Trap

Prior to the chart action depicted above, General Telephone had advanced from 23¾ in October, 1960. In February and March, rallies on volume were stopped at the 30 level, but on April 3 and 4, prices broke through to new highs on volume. (The trap on the Minerals & Chemicals chart was set on the same day.) At this point, the chart analyst normally would interpret the rally as a signal for the next leg of a major advance. However, the rally appeared to peter out, and two weeks later, prices declined below the range of the breakout day, April 3, and into the support zone. This decline closed the trap door and later, when prices closed below the 28 valid support line, the door was locked. The decline from this trap only carried to the 24 level, but the previous support zone became an effective resistance zone. Four rally attempts between July and November were stopped short of this zone.

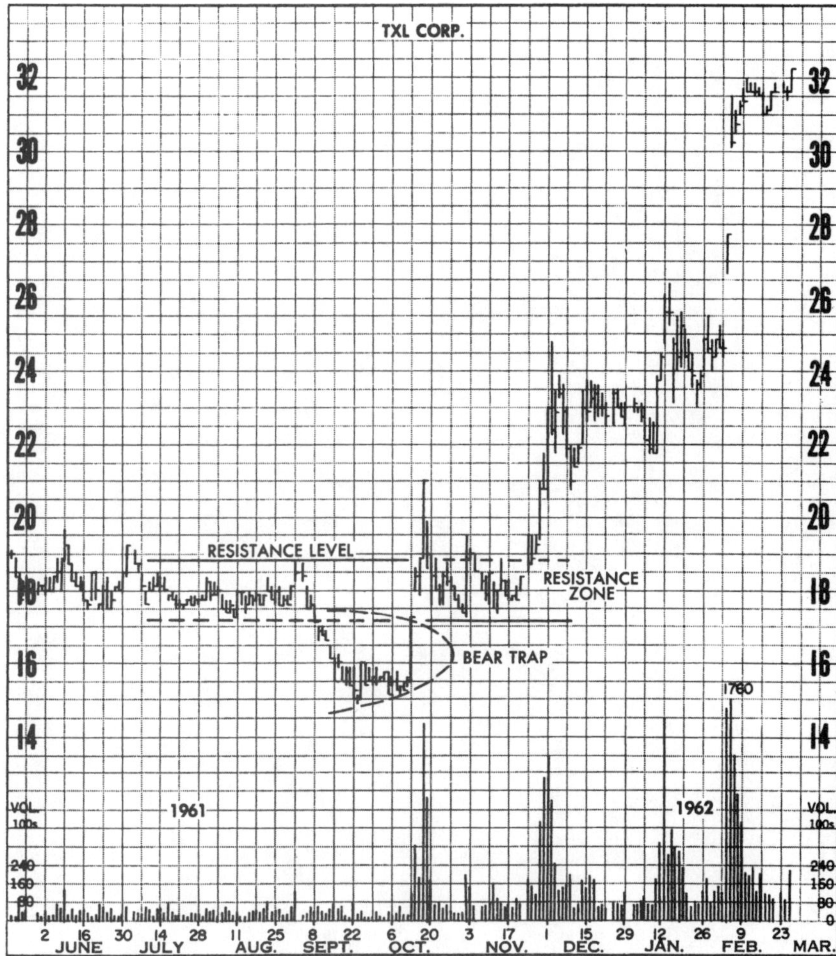

PLATE 50 TXL OIL CORP. — The Bear Trap

The difference between the Bear Trap formation and a number of other reversal configurations that take shape in new low territory lies in the type of congestion that formed prior to the decline to new lows. In the Bear Trap such as outlined on the TXL chart, the chart movements leading to the drop into new lows, outline a sideways trading range of at least several months duration. This is similar to the development of its counterpart, the Bull Trap. However, volume on the drop to new lows in the Bear Trap usually does not expand, while volume may be very high on the rally to new highs in the case of the Bull Trap. One plausible explanation for this difference is the fact that there are far less "bears" or "short sellers" than "bulls" in the market and usually, short sellers are more sophisticated than the average investor. Three of the four trap illustrations in this chapter are Bull Traps because of their much greater frequency of occurrence than Bear Traps.

13

THE MARKET AVERAGES

Up to now, we've been discussing the behavior of individual stocks. But what about "the market" that everybody talks about?

To be sure, nobody literally "plays the market" any more than anybody bets on all the horses in a race; the investor must put his money on individual stocks, not averages. Nevertheless, the public pays a great deal of attention to how the over-all "market" is behaving, as measured by the popular stock averages. When the "market" is going up, the typical shareholder feels encouraged—even if his own stock has declined. And he is not far wrong. As the old Wall Street saying has it, "When they raid the house, they take all the girls—and the piano player." In other words, when the market is in a strong downtrend or uptrend, it will carry with it, sooner or later, a large majority of stocks, including many that, on their own merits, would be behaving quite differently. This makes common sense; obviously, the general attitude of the public toward investment and the business outlook, for example, will affect all individual stocks. Chart analysts have often seen highly bullish patterns of individual stocks disintegrate in a declining market. This usually happens around a turn of the market. A good many stocks *will* buck the market trend, but the odds are, of course, against any individual stock doing so. Hence, no matter what stock an analyst is following, he must at all times be alert for any adverse development in the market as a whole. Put another way, *the market in general is an integral part of the chart analysis of each stock.* Primarily, what the analyst wants to know is whether the market is going through an intermediate "bull" phase or "bear" phase or neutral phase. That is, he is not as concerned with the daily fluctuation of the market, or the historical, years-long trend, as he is with the *intermediate* swings that may move average prices 10 to 25%, and thus materially affect the behavior of the stocks he is working with.

The technical approach to market forecasting—that is, the use of the past and present behavior of the market to predict its future course—dates back before the turn of the century. Its pioneers, Dow, Hamilton and Rhea, based their work on averages or indexes of the prices of selected stocks.

The great popularity of the Dow-Jones averages stems from their writings. The most popular one is, of course, the Dow-Jones Industrials, an average of thirty leading stocks, called industrials primarily to distinguish them from the rails and utilities (although A. T. & T., rather oddly, is listed as an industrial). Although any average based on a limited selection of stocks will be rather sensitive to a wide move in even one issue, the Dow-Jones Industrials has proven to be a thoroughly reliable indicator of the general move-

ment of the market. The New York Times average of twenty-five industrials is also a fairly good yardstick.

The chief reason for using a limited selection to judge the movement of the market as a whole is, of course, convenience. The averages originally were worked out laboriously on pencil and paper. Now, the computer has made possible a much more comprehensive measure. Standard & Poor's uses the 500 leading common stocks on the New York Stock Exchange, representing well over 90% of market values. It multiplies the price of each stock by the number of shares outstanding, then adds all the figures up and reduces them to an index number. And it does so every hour! Even such an index, of course, does not tell everything *about the market. It does not, for example, tell what the* most actively traded *stocks were doing—nor, for that matter, what* your *stock was doing. The analyst should not rely on one source of information about the market and ignore the others. One of them may have something significant to tell him.*

An *average,* roughly speaking, is made by adding up all the prices and dividing by the number of stocks. An *index* takes the sum of prices and compares it with that of a "normal" or base period, usually given as 100. If, for example, the Federal Reserve Board's index of production in a given month is 114, it means production was 14% higher than the average of the base period, which was the year 1957. It should be noted further that, since some stocks are more important than others, and most of them split or issue stock dividends at one time or another, it is necessary to *weight* the averages or indexes to avoid distortion. Occasionally, stocks used in the selected averages must be replaced because of mergers or other changes in the picture.

The basic technique for forecasting the market is a strict chart analysis of one or more of these averages or indexes. *All the chart reading techniques we have discussed in earlier chapters apply just as much to the market as a whole as they do to individual stocks.* There is an additional advantage, in that several market averages are available, so that one may be used to check, or *confirm,* another. A basic tenet of the Dow Theory, for example, is that the Rails must confirm the Industrials (or vice versa) to establish the validity of a trend reversal. This dates back from the days when railroad stocks represented the largest share of all stocks traded; nevertheless, orthodox Dow theorists still insist on such confirmation.

Because of the great sensitivity of the Dow-Jones Industrials to market developments, it may still be regarded as a lead indicator, but confirmation should be looked for in the more comprehensive Standard & Poor's 500, to reduce the possibility of a false signal. And often, the Standard & Poor's index has given the first indication of a new trend's developing, possibly because the Dow-Jones average has been distorted by unusual weakness or strength in one or two heavily weighted stocks. Nevertheless, if Standard & Poor's index points toward a new trend first, confirmation should be sought in the Dow-Jones. Examples of how this confirming technique has actually worked appear in the analyses on the following pages.

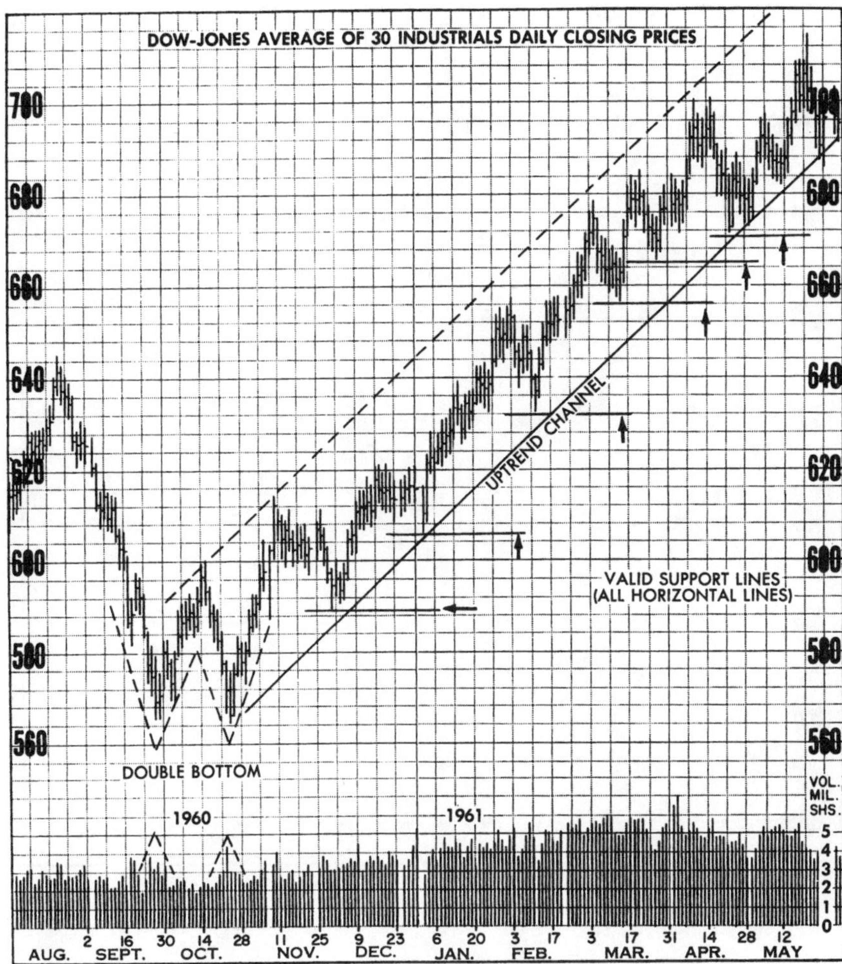

PLATE 51 Analyzing the Daily Chart of the Dow-Jones Average

As explained in Chapter 1, chart analysis techniques apply equally to daily, weekly and monthly range charts and this goes for the various stock averages. The chart above depicts the daily high, low and closing values of the popular Dow-Jones 30 Industrials from August, 1960, to June, 1961. Even though this index is a composite of thirty different stocks, the over-all movement conformed to such ordinary formation development as a Double Bottom, a well-defined uptrend channel and all support and resistance concepts. Close analysis of the uptrend development will reveal that the trendline was slightly penetrated at the end of May, although prices continued to make new highs. This later proved to be a valid caution signal, since the advance eventually bogged down in that approximate area.

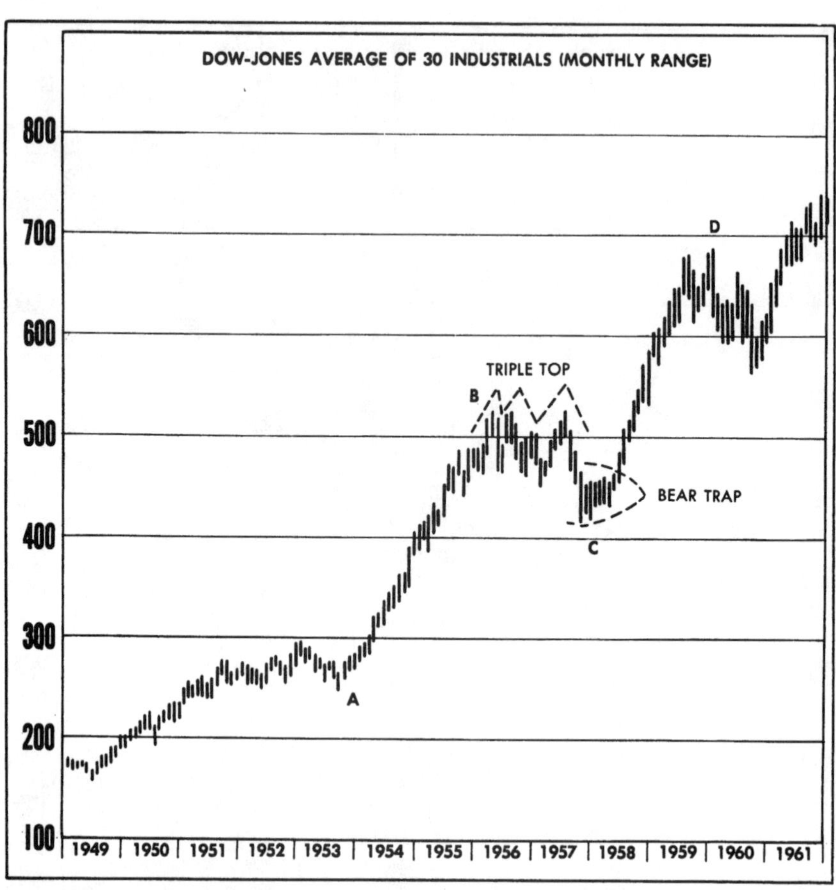

PLATE 52 DOW-JONES AVERAGE — Monthly Ranges 1949-1961

The biggest "bull" market in history (1949-1961) is depicted in chart form by plotting the monthly highs and lows of the Dow-Jones Average of 30 Industrials. It not only shows market history at a glance, but also conforms to fairly normal chart development. Chartists had no difficulty analyzing the trend until 1957 when what appeared to be a Triple Top turned into a Bear Trap. The decline below the 1956 lows had many earmarks of a Triple Top and orthodox chartists would have properly assumed that the picture was bad enough in 1957 to justify liquidation of stocks. However, the rally back into the Triple Top area and through to new highs completed a "Bear Trap" and set a Measured Move in motion. Roughly, the move A to B (250 to 525) could be projected as C to D (415 to 690). Many an experienced chartist who was fooled by the formation could have benefitted greatly by studying other important technical indicators covered in the next chapter.

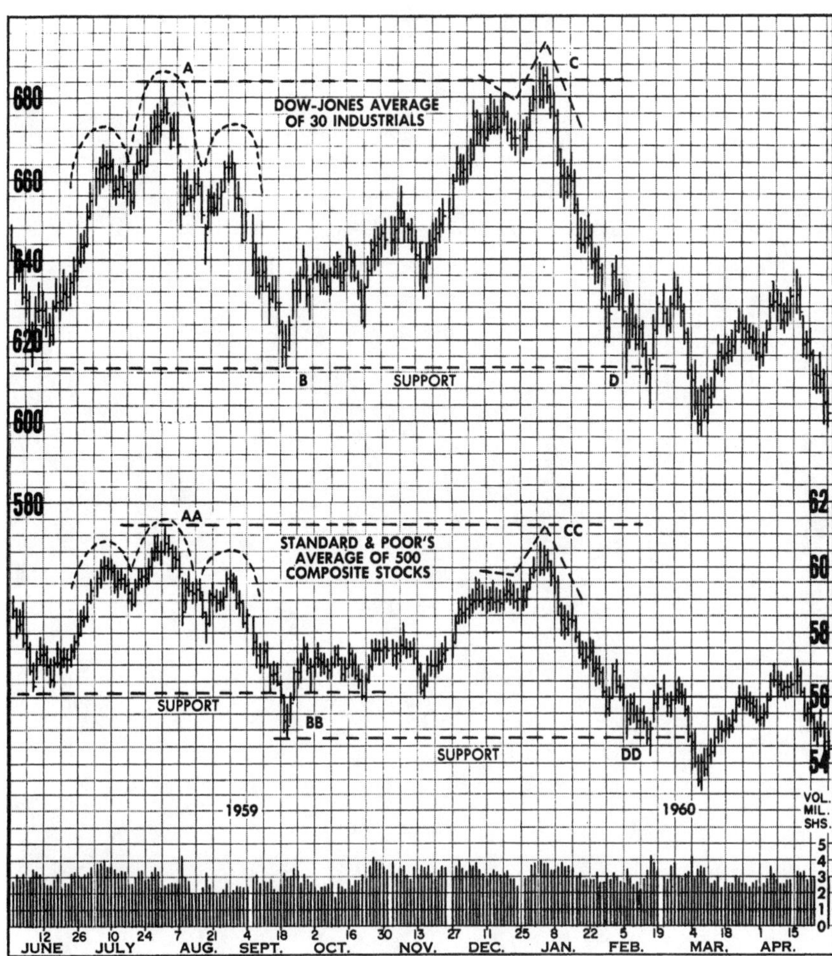

PLATE 53 Dow-Jones Average vs. Standard & Poor's 500

At the end of July, 1959, the Dow-Jones Average of 30 Industrials and the Standard & Poor's Average of 500 Composite Stocks both reached all-time highs. The chart pattern that developed around these historic levels on both averages (A and AA) appeared to be small downsloping Head & Shoulders Tops. The declines from these tops, however, came on very light volume, which detracted from their significance as a possible reversal formation. Then the S & P 500 violated the previous support level (BB), but the D-J Industrials held. This lack of confirmation again suggested that trends were indecisive. Subsequently, the D-J average advanced to a new all-time high (C), but the S & P 500 did not make it (CC). Thus, it refused to confirm the bullish implication of the D-J high. By February (D and DD) both Indexes dropped through major support levels and confirmed a weak price structure. Later in 1960, the D-J Industrials went below 565, S & P 500 declined almost to the 52 level.

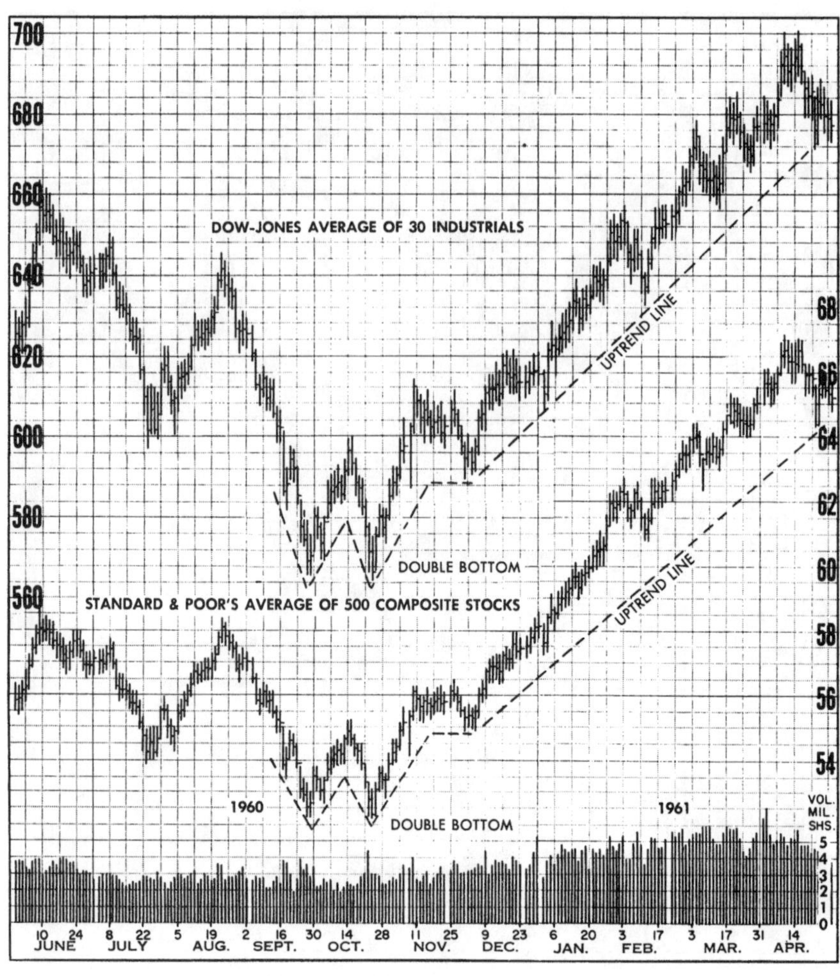

PLATE 54 Dow-Jones Average vs. Standard & Poor's 500

A second chart comparing the movements of the Dow-Jones Average of 30 Industrials and the Standard & Poor Composite Average of 500 stocks is also shown to illustrate the importance of confirmation in chart analysis of the averages. In the chart on the previous page, it was seen how a lack of confirmation pointed to indecisiveness. In the chart above, covering the period June, 1960 to April, 1961, it can be seen that these two averages can move in almost identical fashion. In September, October and November, both averages formed identical almost precise Double Bottom formations (with platform), thus presaging a major move upwards. The advance that followed also proceeded in a duplicate fashion. The only technical difference was the way in which the trendlines formed. The D-J Average adhered closely to a straight line right from the second bottom until April. The S & P 500's trendline was not as well defined.

MORE INDICATORS

In the past forty years or so, a great many techniques have been used in efforts to forecast market trends. Garfield Drew, in his book, "*New Methods for Profit in the Stock Market*," describes and analyzes many of these technical indicators and mechanical systems. It is interesting to note that each of these methods enjoyed some success at one time or another, but no system proved accurate *most of the time*. Joseph Granville, in his book, "*A Strategy of Daily Stock Market Timing for Maximum Profit*" (Prentice-Hall, 1960), also examines many of these indicators and systems, analyzes their successes and failures, and presents a sound approach to the technical study of the market for timing purchases and sales. Some of these methods are well tried, others entirely new, but Mr. Granville's approach is fresh and original. (The author is indebted to him and to Prentice-Hall for much of the material in this and the following chapter.)

The Granville book covers fifty-five basic day-to-day indicators and a number of indicators of intermediate trends, all of which have withstood the test of time. Among the most significant are the Advance-Decline Line, the Short Interest Ratio and Barron's Confidence Index.

ADVANCE-DECLINE LINE

A significant fact about the action of the market that is not closely reflected in the price averages is the number of stocks that go *up* in a given day, as compared with the number that go *down.* It fairly often happens that while the market average is advancing, more individual stocks decline than rise (or vice versa)—either because a few leading stocks are strong, or because the gains are averaging larger than the losses. So analysts have worked up a number of indicators of *breadth,* referring to the number of different stocks that are traded on a given day, and the proportion that rise or fall. These on occasion give an earlier indication of the *underlying strength* of the market more quickly than the price averages, in which the action of a handful of stocks may camouflage the real condition of market psychology.

One of these indicators is the Advance-Decline Line. Granville develops this line by adding up the advances and declines on successive days, and then subtracting the smaller figure from the larger, to get what he calls the "cumulative differential." It's simpler than it sounds, as will be seen from the following hypothetical table showing the first three days of activity (to be continued from day to day). The figures on advances and declines can be obtained, of course, from virtually any newspaper that carries stock-market reports. You can pick any starting date, and keep going, because the real significance of this indicator is in the changing trend, or pattern, rather than the specific numbers charted.

TABLE OF ADVANCES AND DECLINES

	Advances	Declines	Cumulative Advances	Cumulative Declines	Cumulative Differential
Monday	600	400	600	400	+200
Tuesday	525	460	1,125	860	+265
Wednesday	470	510	1,595	1,370	+225

The figures under the column Cumulative Differential are plotted on a chart to produce the Advance-Decline Line.

Granville gives the following principles for interpreting the Advance-Decline Line:

1. When the Dow-Jones Industrial average *falls* while the A-D Line is *rising*, the market will turn *up*.
2. When the Dow-Jones *rises* while the A-D Line *falls*, the market will turn *down*.
3. The strength of such a market rally or reaction will be signalled by how much the price average differs in course from the A-D Line, and for how long.
4. The A-D Line, taken alone, does not indicate *precisely when* such a rally or reaction will occur, but only that it *will* occur reasonably soon.
5. When the Dow-Jones average approaches a previous top and the A-D Line is *below* where it was when it made that top, the market situation is *bearish*. If the A-D Line is *above* where it was when it made that top, a *breakthrough to new highs is imminent*.
6. When the Dow-Jones average approaches a previous low and the A-D Line is well *above* where

it was when it made that low, the market situation is *bullish*—that is, the previous low should hold. But if the A-D Line is *below* where it was when it made that low, then a *downside penetration is imminent.*

The Advance-Decline Line can also be used in conjunction with other market indicators. The reader is urged to develop his own possible uses.

BARRON'S CONFIDENCE INDEX

An interesting effort to measure *confidence* was begun by Barron's Weekly in 1932, and has attracted a considerable following in recent years, thanks largely to Granville's writings. The idea is to get a figure that can be charted, which would show how willing investors are to *take a chance.* Barron's does it by comparing the yield, or rate of return, on high-grade bonds at current market prices with the yield on low-grade bonds. Naturally, yields are higher on the riskier bonds. But when investors grow more confident about the economy, they move from high-grade to lower-grade bonds, and the difference in yields narrows.

What has this to do with the stock market? Well, the theory is that bond buyers are substantial and sophisticated investors—the so-called "smart money." (Actually, they are mostly managers of trusts and large funds.) Their decisions about the economy *today* are likely to be taken up by the general, stock-market public two to four months from now. As a matter of fact, the Confidence Index *has* been tending to *lead* the stock averages by about that length of time—closer to two months than to four of late. Hence, if the Confidence Index tops out and begins to slide, one may look for a similar development in the stock market in 60 to 120 days. Same thing on an upturn, of course.

Caution: The chart interpretation of this index is a bit special. A breakthrough of no more than one-tenth of a point is probably not very significant. What *is* significant is a rally or decline that completes an important chart pattern. Such a development may signal the beginning, or end, of a bull market.

This index has shown a tendency since 1932 to lead the stock market by 60 to 120 days in 85 per cent of the recorded past performance. This means that in 15 per cent of the previous turns the index has either lagged or had a longer lead time, most of those cases showing a longer lead time of 5 or more months. The great years of turn to the downside have fallen into the Confidence Index's 15 per cent time category. In years such as 1929 (adjusted back), 1937 and 1946 the Confidence Index had a lead time of five months or longer. While the Index was trending lower the stock market was rising swiftly and this created a technical tension which ultimately led into an extended decline some months later.

SHORT INTEREST TRENDS AND THE SHORT INTEREST RATIO

If we have an index of confidence, why not an index of pessimism? Well, we have one, indeed. It naturally is based on quite a different breed of operator from the solid, bond-buying citizen whose pulse is taken by Barron's Confidence Index. This different breed is the short seller.

Selling short is a technique most generally used by professional traders and risk-minded investors in an effort to profit by an expected decline in the price of a stock.

(Sometimes, simply to *insure* an investor against a decline, or for tax avoidance purposes, but that's another story.) Anyhow, market analysts agree on a pretty paradox: it is bullish to have plenty of bears around!

There are two reasons for this. One is the theory firmly held by some Wall Street cynics that the public is always wrong—that is, any time *everybody* says the market is going *down,* it will go *up,* and vice versa. The cynics may suggest that, by the time a turn in the economy has seeped down to the general public, it has been anticipated in the market, which already is way ahead on the next bend.

Be that as it may, there's a much more obvious reason, which rests on the nature of short selling. A short *borrows* stock through his broker to sell at the market price. Eventually, he must buy the same number of shares to replace what he has sold. Because he has acted like a bear, he must now behave as a bull. (Every past short sale is a *future* purchase.) Therefore, the *short interest* or *short position* (both are terms for the number of shares sold short but not yet replaced) forms a cushion to stock prices. If they decline, shorts will buy to cash in on their profits. If they go up, shorts may rush to buy to cut their losses.

Thus, a rise in the short interest is bullish, and a decline is bearish. Every investor should watch the short interest in any stock he is following. The leading stock exchanges tabulate the short interest on the 15th of each month. Leading newspapers and financial publications carry these figures a few days later—at least for those stocks in which substantial changes have occurred, or large short positions are outstanding.

The significance of the short position depends on the

volume of trading. Naturally, a short position of 5,000 shares would not be terribly important in a stock that traded 10,000 shares a day, but would be a considerable support to a stock that was trading only 500. Just so, if the market as a whole is very active, even a large short position may not mean much, since the eventual buying that it represents may be quickly satisfied. But in a slow market even a modest short position may set off a sustained rally.

The Short Interest Ratio, therefore, is the ratio of the short interest (or position) to the average daily volume for a given month. For example, if the short interest totals 4,000,000 shares and the volume of trading is averaging 3,500,000 shares a day, the Short Interest Ratio is about 1.14.

As a general rule, whenever the Short Interest Ratio rises above 1.5, the market is likely to be in an "oversold" position and the outlook is bullish. When the Ratio falls below .5, the market's position has been greatly weakened and an important downturn is indicated. The "in-between" readings of 1.0 to 1.5 should be regarded as slightly bullish, while .5 to 1.0 may be considered as a caution zone.

TRENDLINE'S ODD-LOT INDEX

Another indicator that has been drawing a growing following is also based, in a sense, on the theory that the majority is always wrong. It may be suggested that, by the time a new trend or development has seeped down to the "little fellow," the "smart money" has already acted on it, and is looking forward to the next development—just as the "taste makers" set a new fashion, and then drop it by the time the general public has picked it up. (Remember when automobiles ballooned out, and tailfins were at their gaudiest? The "taste makers" already were driving little foreign cars, and a social analyst could have predicted that compact cars for the masses were just around the corner.)

As it happens, the market offers a keen measurement of the attitude of the "little fellow." This is the volume of trading in odd lots—or lots of less than 100 shares. In round lots, there is a seller for every buyer. But odd lots are purchased from, or sold to, jobber firms that keep a supply in inventory, and serve other brokers by buying or selling odd lots at a fraction of a point above or below the market price. Daily, they report how many shares have been bought and sold (including how many have been sold short). Thus, we know whether the "little fellow" is selling more stock than he's buying, or vice versa, and to what extent.

Garfield Drew has been credited with refining a technique for forecasting the market by use of the figures on odd-lot trading, on the assumption that the odd-lot trader is always wrong. The Trendline Corp., leading publisher of stock market charts, found on careful research that there was much validity in this approach. It developed Trendline's Odd-Lot Index to show the odd-lot trend at a glance. This was computed as follows:

1. The weekly ratio of odd-lot purchases to odd-lot sales was studied for the twenty-four years 1937 through 1960. It was confirmed that odd-lotters normally buy more shares than they sell (partly, perhaps, because they sometimes accumulate stock until they get round lots, and partly simply because the market has been expanding, and rising over the long haul).

2. This normal ratio—11 to 10—was established as the *normal buying line.*
3. On a chart, each week's ratio is plotted in relation to the normal buying line.
4. The index is seasonally adjusted during the period between November 1 and January 20 of each year. It was found that odd-lot buying, in relation to selling, drops off sharply from November 1 to December 20—and it picks up sharply from December 20 to January 20.

Obviously, when the index is above the normal buying line, odd-lotters are buying more than they usually do, and when it is below the line, they are buying less than they usually do. Research over many years has produced the following principles for interpreting the index:

1. Odd-lot buying is invariably much less than normal during a bull move. This can help to confirm a rise in the market as a valid major move.
2. Toward the *end of an advance,* odd-lotters begin to buy more than normally. They continue to do so while the market is making its top. Often their buying becomes frenzied close to the very top.
3. They also buy more than normally during the beginning stage of a decline in the market. This tapers off as the decline continues.
4. Around a valid bottom, odd-lot buying is usually well below normal.

No one index, method or system has ever forecast the market with complete accuracy. However, intelligent judgment of the methods outlined in this chapter, taken together, can raise one's batting average enormously.

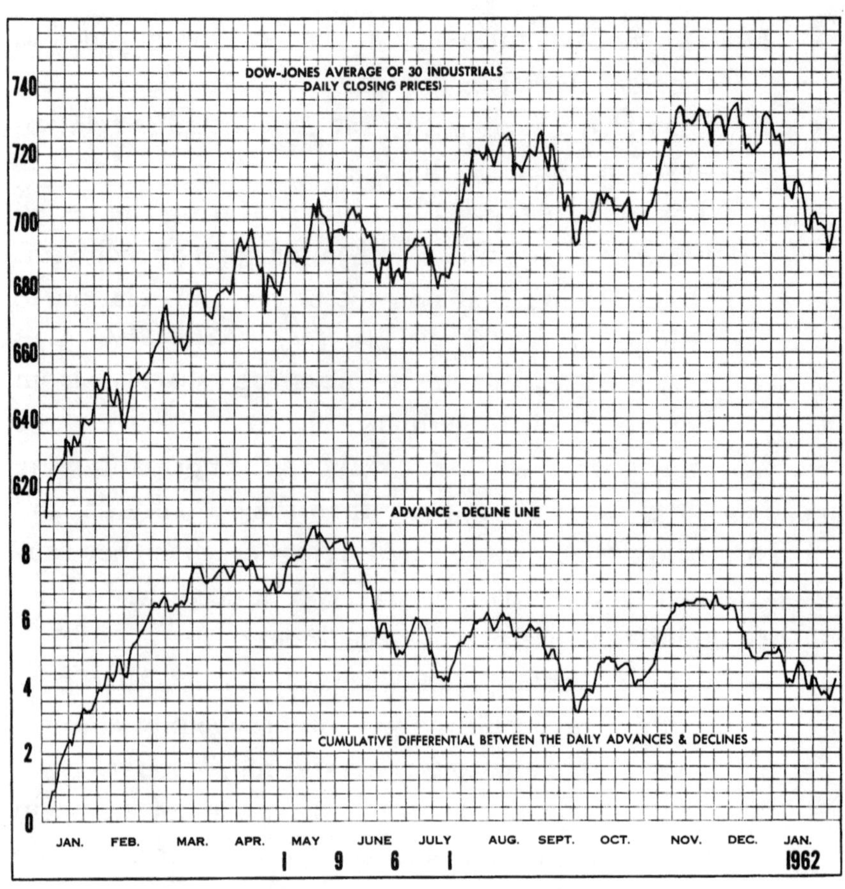

PLATE 55 The Advance-Decline Line

Analysis of any one indicator must always be considered in conjunction with as many other indicators as possible. In addition, the rules suggested in the text for interpreting the various indicators are merely guidelines and not dogma. Examination of the chart of the Advance-Decline Line for 1961 and through January 1962, discloses that a vigorous uptrend at the beginning of 1961 set the pace for a rising Dow-Jones Index. The A-D Line topped out in June, 1961, and although the D-J Index continued to make new highs, the down-turn in the A-D Line served as a warning to the technician that the averages were not likely to get far. A slowing down of the advance and the decline in January 1962 validated this reasoning. During the greater part of 1961, the A-D Line appeared to be far more indicative of the trend of the broad market than the Dow-Jones Average, or for that matter, other leading stock averages as well.

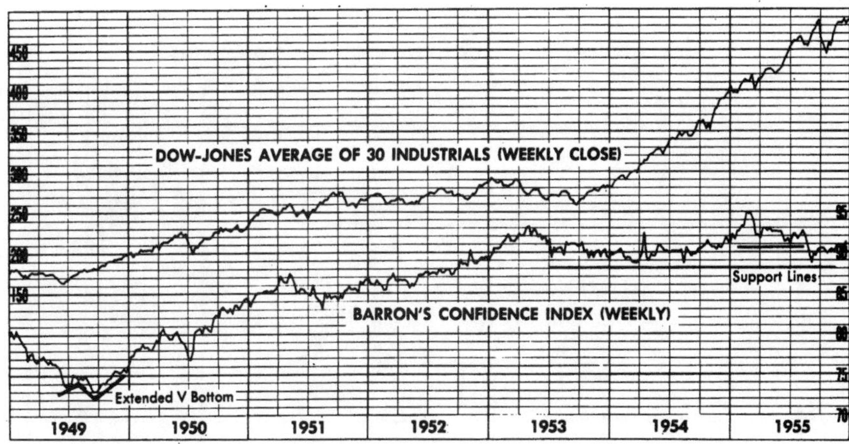

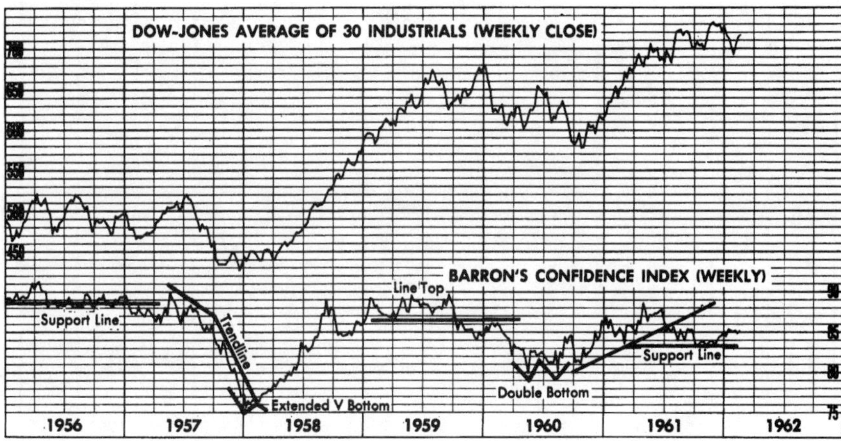

PLATE 56 Barrons' Confidence Index

Most of the adherents of the use of the Confidence Index wait for minor moves in the Index as indications of forthcoming minor moves in the stock market averages. The writer prefers a different kind of utilization of the Index, i.e., to consider the Index itself as a subject for chart analysis. Outlines of major formations which seem to be significant in forecasting trends of the Confidence Index and the averages are marked on the charts above. The V Bottom in 1949 heralded the long "bull" market and no major top formation could be seen until 1956 and 1957, when important support zones were violated. The index traced a downcurving trendline, climaxed by an Extended V Bottom in January 1958. A Line Top in 1959 set a decline in motion which was reversed by a Double Bottom in 1960. The trend was higher until June when an uptrend line was broken; however, the support line along the Jan.-Mar. low was not decisively broken so that a major "bear" signal was deferred.

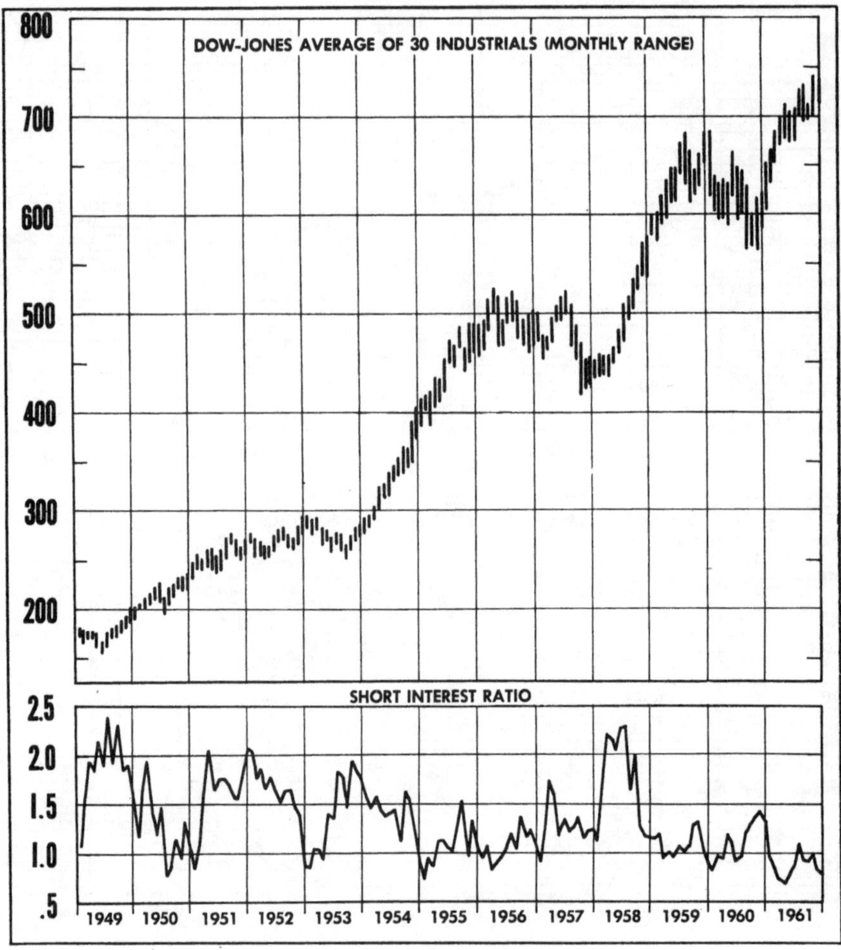

PLATE 57 Short Interest Ratio and the D-J Industrials

The explanation of how to use the Short Interest Ratio indicated that the market outlook is bullish when the ratio is over 1.5. In studying the relationship of the D-J monthly chart and the Short Interest Ratio line, between 1949 and 1961 this rule proved to be especially effective. A look at the chart might suggest an amendment to the general rules, i.e., "over 2.0, the situation is extremely bullish." This occurred in 1949 and 1958. It will be recalled from the previous chapter that the chart picture in early 1958 was particularly bearish, but the implied bullishness of this indicator at that time should have helped to nullify any bearish chart interpretation to a great degree. The reading may be considered as "bearish" when the line drops below .5, although as low as .5 to 1.0 may be considered a caution zone. Throughout the period of this chart the indicator held well above the bearish or "overbought" zone.

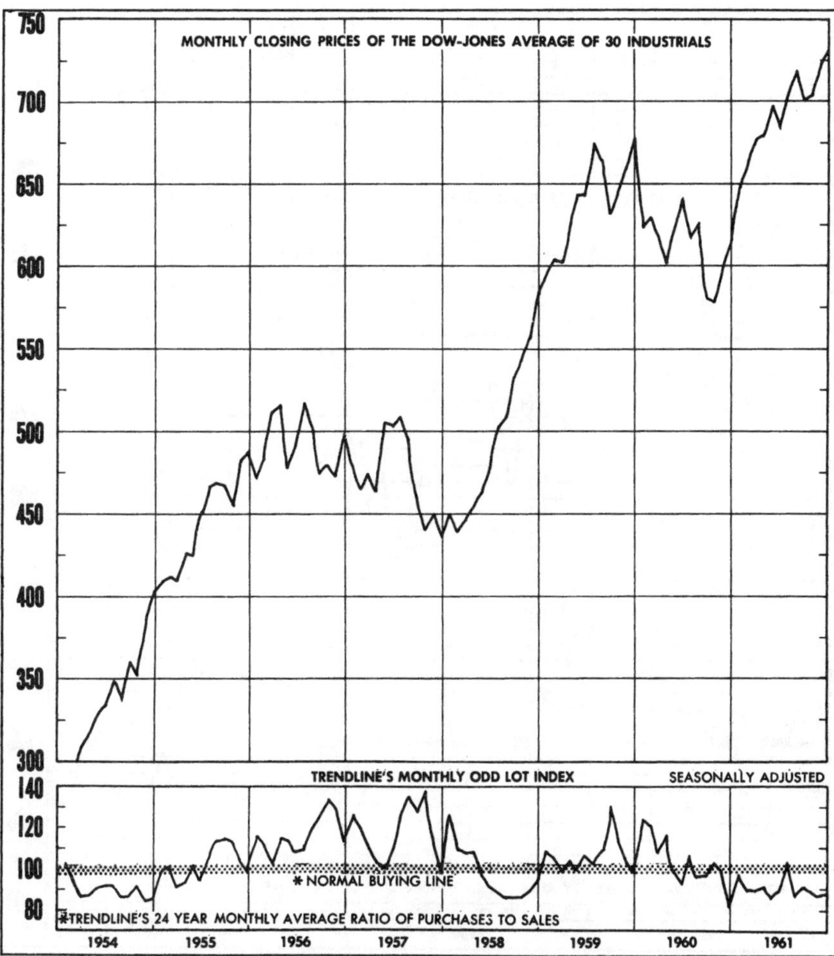

PLATE 58 Trendline's Monthly Odd Lot Index and the Dow-Jones Average

A comparison of Trendline's Odd Lot Index and the Dow-Jones Average of 30 Industrials on this and the following page will reveal how the Odd Lot Index helped to anticipate major turns in the Dow-Jones Average, and confirm the existence of genuine "bull" moves. For a long-range perspective, the Odd Lot Index and the Dow-Jones Average were plotted on a monthly basis. It can be seen that the odd lot purchases remained under the Normal Buying Line (NBL) throughout 1954 and most of 1955 (which was "bullish"), and the Average moved sharply higher without interruption. Odd lot buying in 1956 was above the NBL and the advance in the Average bogged down. In 1956 and 1957, the Odd Lot Index jumped well above normal, a "bearish" indication, and the Average was mostly reactionary. In 1958, odd lot buying was considerably below normal and the Average again rallied vigorously. The analysis for 1959, 1960 and 1961 is covered on the following page.

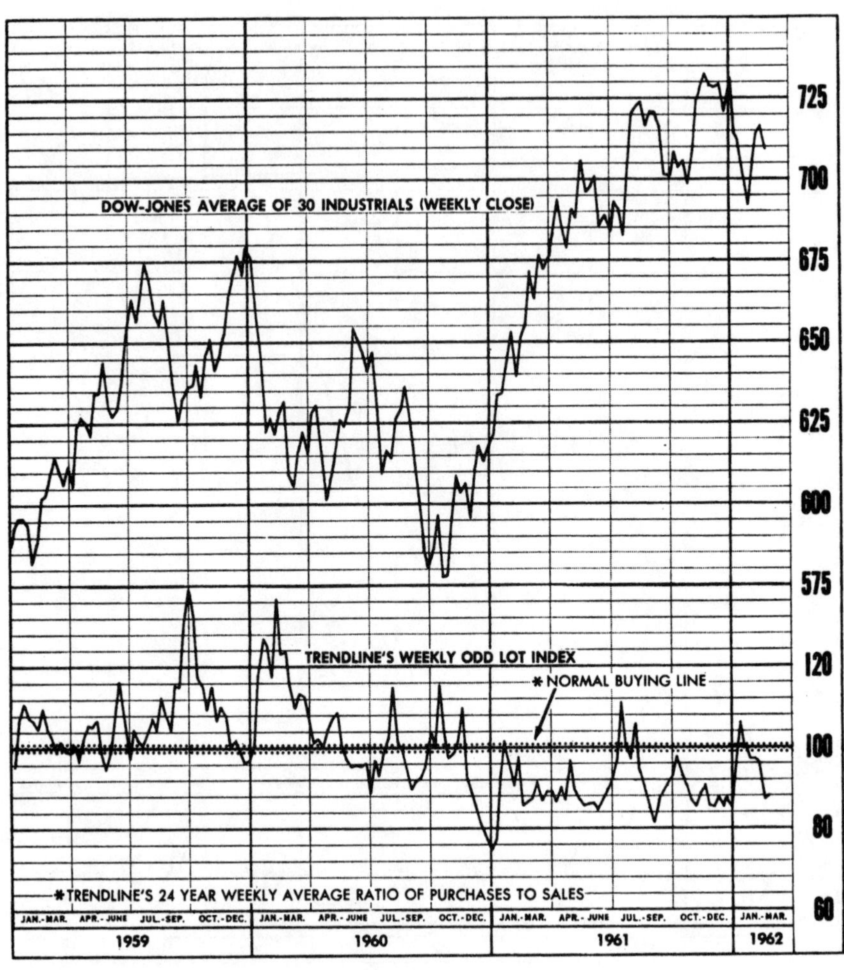

PLATE 59 Trendline's Weekly Odd Lot Index and the Dow-Jones Average

For a closer analysis (than the preceding page), the Trendline's Odd Lot Index and the Dow-Jones Industrial Average are plotted on a weekly basis for the years 1959, 1960 and 1961. This chart will show how wide changes in the Odd Lot Index affected subsequent minor movements in the Average. In September, 1959, abnormal odd lot buying after a sharp stock market reaction was immediately followed by an advance in the Average. Another odd lot buying bulge after a sharp market decline in January and February, 1960, appeared to lead to a market advance several months later. However, in both cases, the Odd Lotters proved to be on thin ice as each price advance quickly gave way to new lows. Then in December, 1960, odd lot buying dropped way below normal, and this signaled the important stock market advance of 1961. Further confirmation of a continuing "bull" move was evidenced by the odd lot buying pattern in 1961 which was generally maintained below normal.

15

THE "200 DAY MOVING AVERAGE"

Stock market technicians have experimented over the years with any number of methods for detecting or measuring trends. Many use some kind of *moving average,* in an effort to iron out the daily fluctuations. For example, an economist working with the monthly figures on new building contracts may want to smooth out the trend line in order to reduce the distortion that a single big contract may introduce into a month's volume. He may then use a three-month moving average—that is, to get a working figure for March, he will *average* the actual figures for February, March and April. His working figure for April will be the March-April-May average, and so on. He can plot such a series on a chart, and obtain quite a reliable trend line. Similar techniques have their place in market analysis. The Advance-Decline Line, described in the preceding chapter, is one kind of moving average.

One advantage of such an average as a measure of trends is that it is produced by a simple arithmetical computation and does not depend on personal judgment.

The moving average that covers about 200 days has won great favor among analysts as a measurement of long-range trends. The most laborious way to set one up is to add up the closing prices of a stock (or market average) on 200 consecutive days, then divide by 200 to get the moving average for the 200th day. On the 201st day, Day No. 1 is dropped and the price for Day No. 201 is added. And so on.

Most analysts, including Granville, find it just as satisfactory and less tedious to use one price a week for thirty weeks. The Trendline Corporation computes its "200-day moving averages" by adding the closing prices of thirty consecutive Thursdays, and dividing by thirty. Each week, the new figure is added, and the one for thirty weeks earlier is dropped. Such an average is customarily plotted on regular stock price charts, for comparison with daily price developments.

Granville lists eight basic rules for interpreting such charts:

1. If the 200-day average line *flattens out* or *advances* following a decline, and the price of the stock penetrates that average line on the upside, this constitutes a major buying signal.
2. If the price of the stock falls below the average line while the average line is still *rising*, this also is a buying signal.
3. If the stock price is above the 200-day line and declines toward it, but fails to go through and instead turns up again, this is a buying signal.
4. If the stock price falls too fast and far below a declining average line, a short-term rebound

toward the line may be expected.

5. If the average line flattens out or declines following a rise, and the stock price penetrates that line on the downside, this constitutes a major selling signal.
6. If the price of the stock rises above the average line while the average line is still *falling*, this also is a selling signal.
7. If the stock price is below the average line and rises toward it, but fails to go through and instead turns down again, this is a selling signal.
8. If the stock price rises too fast above a rising average line, a short-term reaction may be expected.

It should be emphasized that these guidelines should not be used as a "system" for playing the market, but merely as another technical tool—a handy addition to the basic techniques of chart analysis. The daily price action should be given first consideration, especially in timing market turns. The 200-day moving average is *not* a sensitive indicator, and trend reversals often are clearly outlined in the price action well before the moving average itself turns.

Keeping abreast of the various indicators is a comparatively simple matter inasmuch as they are published in chart form on a continuous basis. The weekly publication, "DAILY BASIS STOCK CHARTS," published by Trendline Corp., 82 Beaver Street, New York 5, N. Y., provides up-to-date charts each week on the Advance-Decline Line, Trendline's Odd-Lot Index, Barron's Weekly Confidence Index and the Short Interest Ratio. This interesting publication also charts the daily fluctuations of the Dow-Jones

Industrials and Standard & Poor's 500-Stock Average and shows the 200-day moving average line for these latter two indices. In addition, the hundreds of charts for individual stocks that are published weekly, include a 200-day moving average line on each chart.

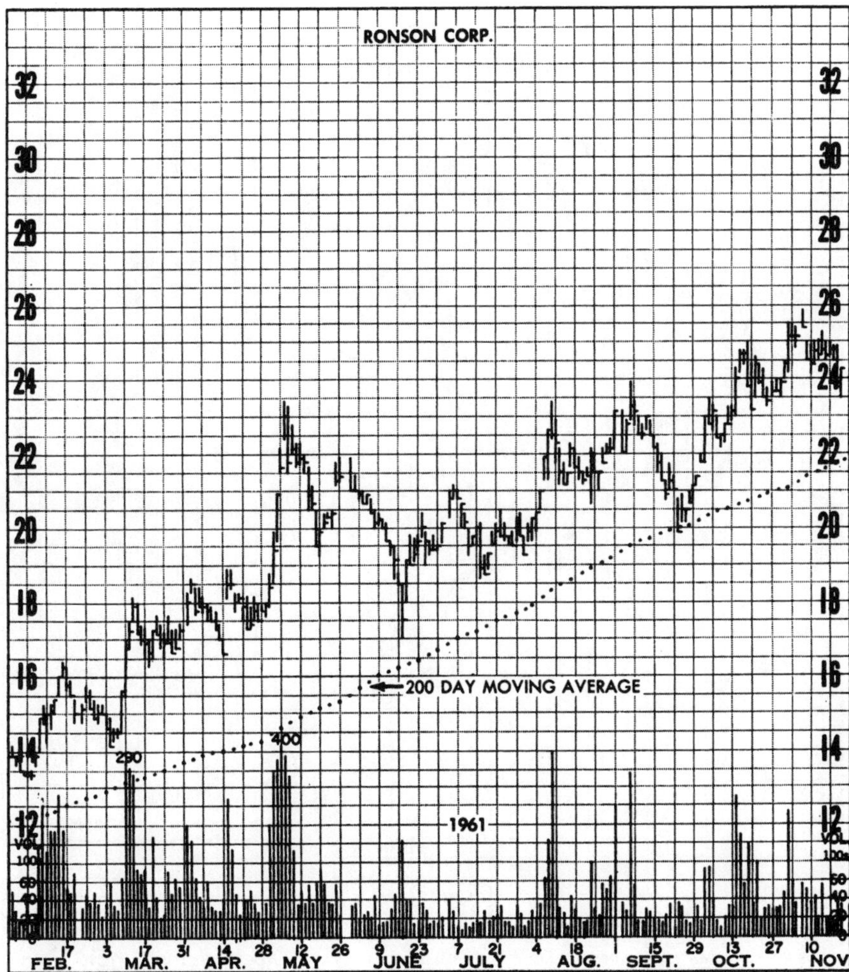

PLATE 60 RONSON — 200-Day Moving Average and Price Move Up Together

During "bull" moves prices usually hold above their 200-Day Moving Average. In the chart above, prices and the 200-Day Moving Average moved upward in rather close order. The rally in early May was the only instance when prices rallied out of line with the moving average, and this proved to be of short duration. In this situation, the moving average was easily the best indicator of trend development. The drawing of trendlines and even the support and resistance concepts could have been misleading to the chart technician but, throughout the advance, the moving average left no doubt about the direction prices were moving. As stated in this chapter, the moving average is a "handy addition to the basic techniques of chart analysis", and it will be seen in this and the examples that follow, at times it can be the main technical tool.

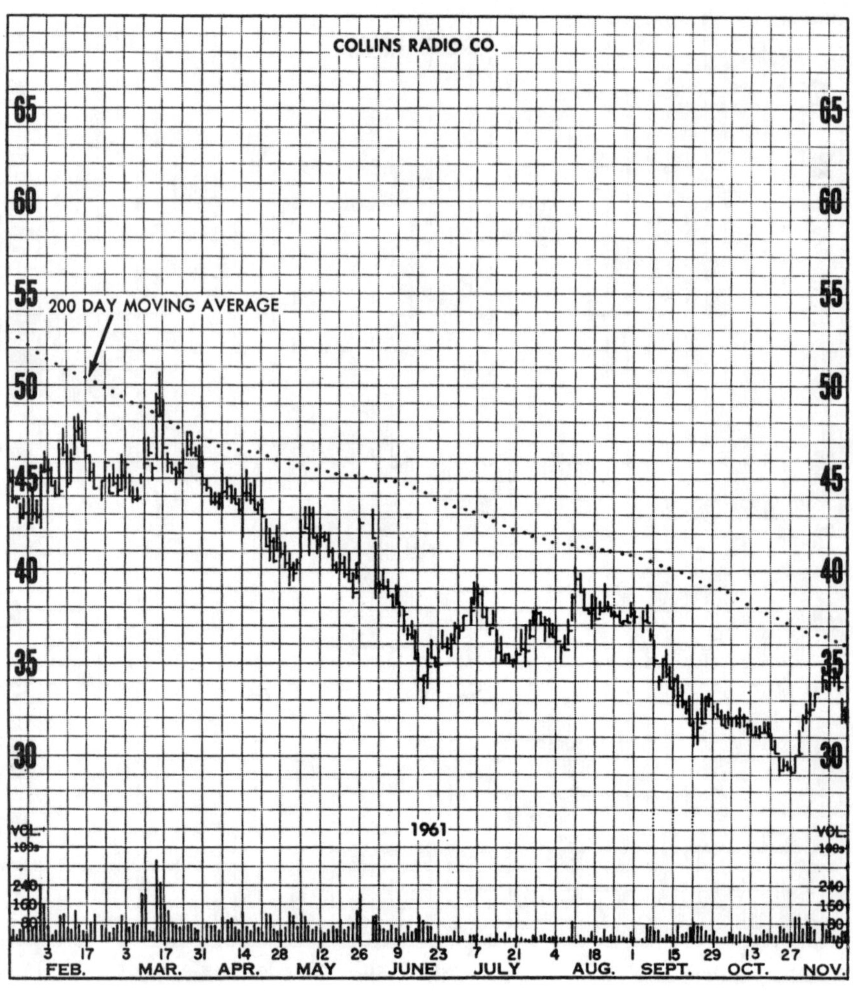

PLATE 61 COLLINS RADIO —
200-Day Moving Averages and Prices Move Lower Together

This chart picture looks almost like an upside down "mirror image" of the preceding Ronson Chart. In downtrends, prices remain below the moving average. The attraction of prices to the moving average can be just as strong in a downtrend as in an uptrend. This chart shows another case where the moving average proved to be the primary technical tool. Most experienced chart analysts would otherwise have heen fooled by the March rally, which broke through two previous resistance levels. But, Granville's Rule 6 says, "If the price of the stock rises above the average line while the average is still falling, this also is a selling signal". When strict chart interpretation becomes clouded (as it often does), the moving average is a welcome addition to the technician's tool kit.

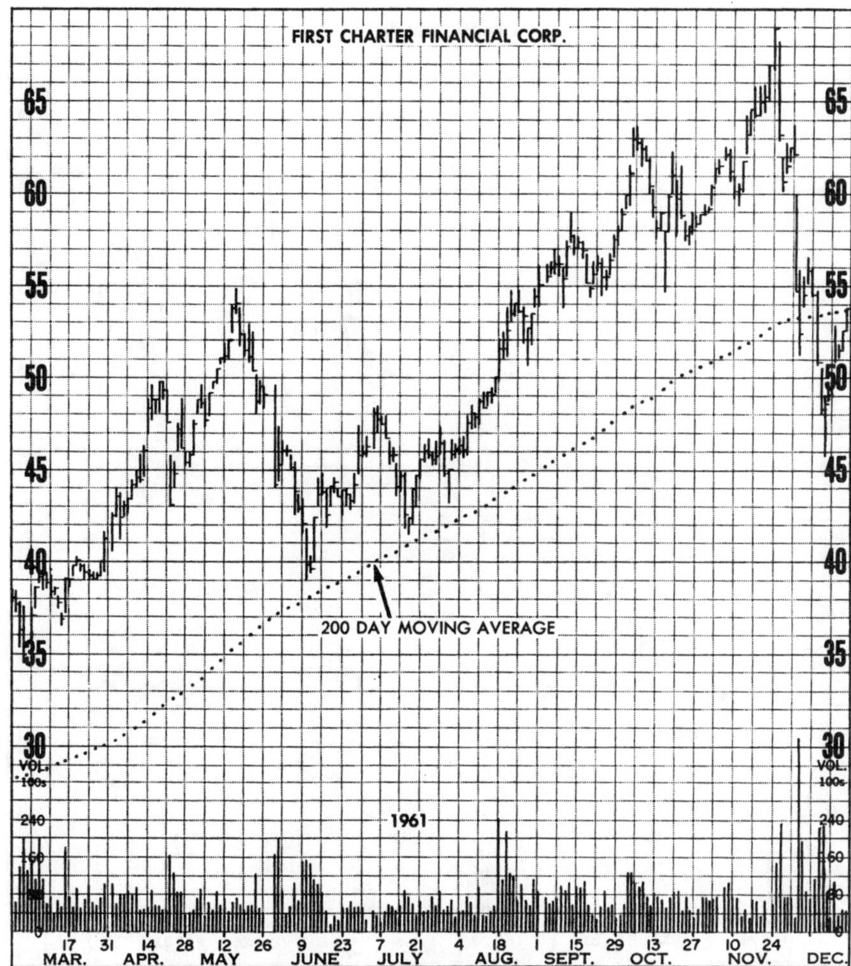

PLATE 62 FIRST CHARTER FINANCIAL —
Return Moves To 200-Day Moving Average

Granville's Rule 8 states, "If the stock price rises too fast above a rising moving average line, a short-term reaction may be expected". This rule would have been extremely helpful to the short-term trader in this illustration. At the 55 level in May, the stock was 19 points above the average line, three weeks later, a reaction of 16 points had carried it back nearly to the moving average. The pattern was repeated in November and December—with two important differences. Note how the 16-point reaction in May and June occurred on light volume and stopped short of the average line. In November and December, volume picked up sharply on the decline and prices went through the average line on continued high volume. This should have warned the chartist that this second reaction was not a routine move, but a significant turn in trend.

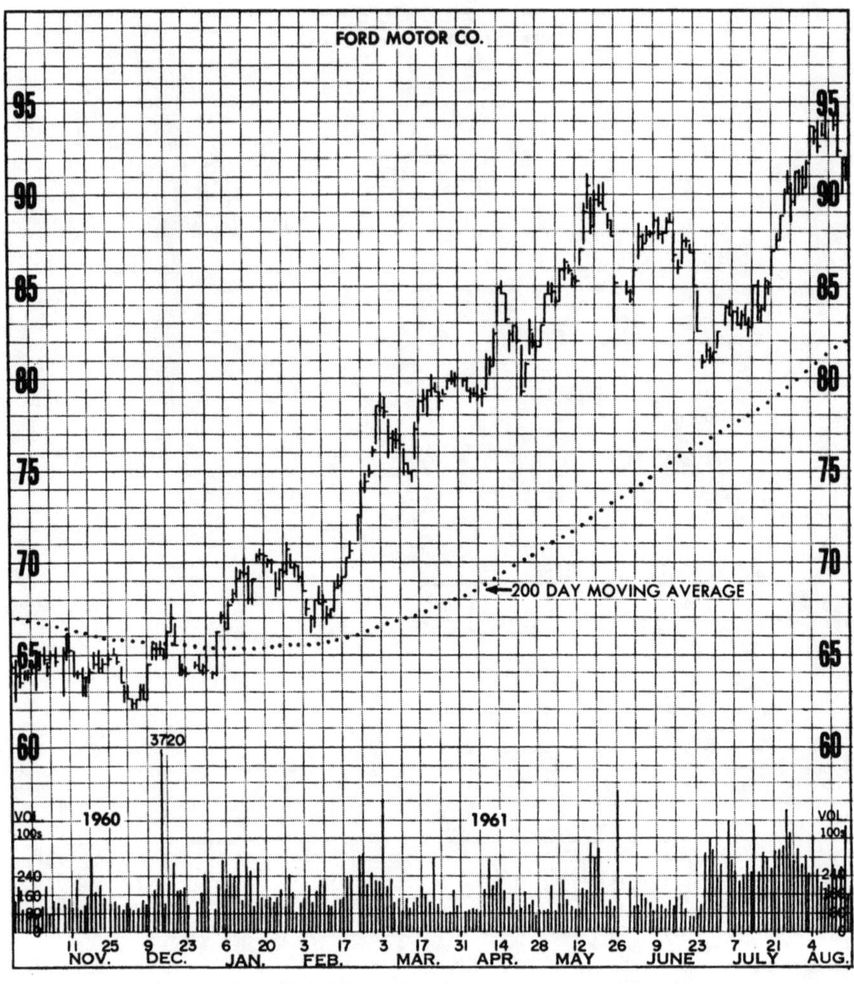

PLATE 63 FORD MOTOR CO.
200-Day Moving Average Signaling Major Bottom

In the second week of January, 1961, prices rallied over an important resistance level (68½) and established an uptrend line. This rally also penetrated the moving average line for the second time in three weeks. Considering Granville's Rule 1, "If the 200-Day Moving Average line flattens out or advances following a decline, and the price of the stock penetrates that average line on the upside, this constitutes a major buying signal", this penetration (or the one three weeks before) could be interpreted as such a signal. Research in the past several years has indicated that this rule and Rule 5 (relating to major selling signals) can be subject to many false moves and misinterpretation. It is suggested that, before regarding a penetration of the "average" line as a major buy or sell signal, confirming signals should also be found in the independent action of the price chart.

PROFITS

The able student of the charts will be right about the market more often than he is wrong. That should be enough to make a profit, but even an exceptional ability to predict stock prices by no means automatically assures success in the marketplace. Forecasting is one thing, trading another. As an oldtime Wall Streeter said, "Forecasting sows the seed; trading reaps the harvest." A sound forecast tells you a stock is going up, but it takes proper trading *tactics* to determine how much money to risk, at what moment, and when to get out. A good forecaster can go broke, if he is a poor trader, while some good traders who were poor forecasters have become rich. There are in fact many brilliant analysts in Wall Street who have never made money in the market. A friend of mine says of such people, "They have good heads, but holes in their shoes." Chart reading must be married to a sound trading or investment program to mend those shoes.

Wall Street writers love to discuss market operations in military terms. A best-seller is called "The Battle for

Investment Survival" (by Gerald Loeb). One hears the market called a "battlefield," with "buying and selling forays" and "bull and bear raids." In line with this war talk, we might say that chart techniques and other means of analyzing company prospects are all fine weapons, but good tactics are needed to win battles. A proper investment program can't be taught in a book; it must be tailored to suit each individual's personality and pocketbook. We'll try here to offer a few guidelines.

To begin with, one must have a plan of action. Any plan is better than none. Your plan might be devised out of the answers to the following questions:

1. How much do you have to invest?
2. How much are you prepared to lose?
3. What are your investment objectives?
4. How do you get in?
5. How do you get out?

1. *How much do you have to invest?* The prospective investor should *not* touch the funds needed for the basics of life, such as housing, insurance, a cash reserve adequate for regular and emergency expenses, and a minimum set aside for retirement. One of Bernard Baruch's cardinal rules was, "never commit all of your funds to the market." Furthermore, it's a good idea not to commit all of your available *investment* funds. For example, if you have $20,000 left, after deducting those basic needs, it may be wise to commit anywhere from 10% to 90% in the market at various times,

depending on opportunities and your analysis of market conditions. Before committing the greater share of your funds, you should have a good backlog of profits and be extremely optimistic about the general market outlook. That extra cash position will provide maneuverability and help you maintain an objective viewpoint, which is vital to market analysis.

2. *How much are you prepared to lose?* To the unsophisticated investor, "lose" is a dirty word. The experienced investor knows that any situation can turn sour. Just as Napoleon always allowed for a margin of error on the battlefield, you must allow for market adversity. A good business man must determine in advance how much risk he is willing to run, and how much loss he is willing to take, before retreating. The market will always be there; if you want to live to fight another day, you must know when to say "enough." The odds favor the sound analyst—but only if he does not go broke on one or two investments that will show a loss. One successful trading program that comes to mind uses a 10% rule. If a stock purchase goes the wrong way, the trader gets out when the loss hits 10%. He either gives his broker a *stop-loss order* (a standing order to sell his stock at the market if it falls to a certain point) or he gives himself a mental stop order—which, by the way, requires great self-discipline. Other traders allow themselves a range of possible loss up to 25%, which may be reasonable, taking into

account one's resources, tax situation, profit backlog and other considerations.

3. *What are your investment objectives?* Once you know how much you are going to commit and how much loss you are willing to risk, you should have a good idea of what your objectives are. You may set yourself a goal of a 25% profit on an investment, 50% or even 100%—keeping in mind that, generally speaking, the greater the risk the greater the potential profit, and vice versa. You may prefer simply to ride with the trend, *pyramiding*—that is, buying more stock as the price moves up. Such a method must be protected by an automatic way of getting out of the market, such as stop-loss orders that are kept a certain distance below the price as it rises. You may reject either of these approaches, and rely simply on chart analysis to determine when to get out. Whatever method you use, you should have an objective in mind before you invest, and stick to it.
4. *How do you get in?* Your attention may be drawn to a particular stock in any number of perfectly valid ways. It may be that you like a company's product or admire its management—or you may have received a tip. There is nothing wrong with looking into a tip from a reliable source, but it's a grievous error to buy a stock merely because you've had a tip. (Also, as the famous trader Jesse Livermore put it, "If you buy on Smith's tip, you must sell on Smith's tip.") You should find out everything you can about the stock. Read the

company's reports and Prospectuses, the data in Moody's or Standard & Poor's, and any studies put out by brokerage houses or investment advisory firms. You may even write the company for information. Do as complete an analysis as you can of its sales, profits, cash flow (profits plus depreciation) and other fundamental information. *Then study the chart.* If the construction is basically bullish, and your other analyses agree, the odds will greatly favor an investment. Again, the chart should be consulted to find the best time to buy—at a breakout point, a support level, or a normal reaction on light volume. At this point, you must take your position. You should determine how much money you will commit on this stock and whether you will do it all at once or piecemeal, buying on reactions, or on the "scale-up" —that is, buying additional shares as and if the market rises. *Never buy on the scale-down.* If you do that, you will only compound your losses. Mathematically, that shifts the odds against you, unless you have an awful lot of faith, an awful lot of nerve and an awful lot of money.

5. *How do you get out?* This is undoubtedly the hardest part of any investment program. The common laments of Wall Street operators, professional and amateur alike, are, "I should have sold while I was ahead!" and "I should have hung on a little longer!"

   Here again, you must have an objective, and a plan of action. If your investment system tends toward the mechanical, you may decide that (A) you are willing to assume a 10% loss in any investment; (B) you figure to be right only once out of three times; hence (C) you must clear well more than 30% when you *are* right to make a net profit. Some traders set a fixed goal of 50% or 100% or whatever. One recent best-seller on the market claimed that enormous profits were made by a system of trailing stop-loss orders. The author would keep raising his stop-loss price under congestion areas, which he called "boxes of price action." He would get out automatically on abnormal reactions. Of course, this assured that he would always be sold out somewhere *below* the top, but as Bernard Baruch says in his autobiography, "Only liars sell at tops and buy at bottoms." A pure chartist, on the other hand, uses chart techniques to determine when to get out of the market. He sells when his analysis indicates that an advance is slowing down, or that a reversal is imminent or already getting under way. To wait for confirmation of a reversal is an excellent method, but it requires great self-discipline, and some people will never be objective enough to employ this approach.

To repeat: *any plan is better than no plan.* Also, an investment plan is a highly personal thing. You must know your own weaknesses and strengths, and adopt a plan that not only meets your needs, but also is one you can live with. The writer recently came across a strikingly similar thought in the writings of two famous stock market operators. One said the most important thing one could learn about the stock market was to "know thyself." The other said, "If there is any key to the process of growing up, it lay in the systematic effort of critical self-appraisal. And as I came to know myself, I acquired a better understanding of other people."

Aside from your own foibles, of course, your financial condition, the amount of time you can devote to the market and your experience are important in devising an investment program.

PITFALLS — AND PROFITS

Chart reading is an art, not a science, and many a pitfall awaits the investor who forgets this. Let us review some of its limitations:

Bombshells: Dynamic unexpected events can reverse chart trends without warning. These may be war scares, "peace scares," or surprise action by the government affecting market sentiment in general; they may be bonanzas or disasters affecting a single company or industry. Wall Street vividly remembers the first session after President Eisenhower's heart attack in 1956, when billions of dollars in market values were wiped out in hours. Proxy fights, antitrust actions, new products, mergers often dramatically alter trends. Chart analysis is based on market psychology, not hocus-pocus, and it is nonsense to believe, as some "pure" theorists appear to do, that *all* events are written in the charts before they occur. The chart, in short, is not an Ouija board.

Indecisions, indecisions: Stocks have been said to spend two-thirds of the time making up their minds what they will do in the remaining third of the time. The experienced chartist will heartily concur. Frequently, he is asked, "What does the chart say?" Often, the answer is: "Nothing." (However, while *most* stocks are giving no signal whatever most of the time, *some* stocks are always on the move, or getting ready to move.) The analyst with access to many charts will find plenty of promising trends or formations.

No two are alike: It is part of the attraction of the market that every situation, like every person, is at least a little different from all others. Since no two patterns form in exactly the same manner, their interpretation depends on the experience, judgment and imagination of the chartist. Granville compares chart reading to piano playing. Anybody can learn to follow the notes on the score, more or less, but what comes out is something else again. As the little old lady said to the boy who asked her how to get to Carnegie Hall: "Practice! Practice!"

Wha' Hoppen? Sometimes, what seems to be a confirmed, clearly established formation or trend will suddenly fall apart without any apparent reason. Even a post-mortem may not show why. Admittedly, this doesn't happen often; good old hindsight will usually find what went wrong. But it happens.

Quirks: Many stocks have personalities of their own, and tend to repeat certain patterns—or to behave too erratically to follow, in which case the analyst will say, "This stock just doesn't chart well." One stock may regularly form double tops or bottoms: another may prefer rounding turns to saucer bottoms; a third may turn on a dime. There is nothing particularly spooky about this. A stock very likely will attract a special kind of market following, which will behave in a certain way. Also, a company may be affected by a cycle all its own, or it may be subject to erratic swings in earnings. This individual personality of stocks is listed here as a *pitfall,* but it is also an *opportunity.* The investor who is familiar with the longterm behavior of a stock can call a turn with increased confidence.

Tidal Waves: As we have said before, the most clearly defined patterns of individual stocks will disintegrate without warning in a general turn of the market. Hence, the sound analyst closely follows general market conditions, both technical and economic.

CONCLUSION

If we have emphasized the limitations of chart analysis, it is partly because we recall the disrepute into which the charts—and everything else about the stock market fell after the 1929 crash. In some brokerage houses, analysts had to hide their charts for fear of ridicule or banishment! That has, of course, long since changed. Nowadays, charts are studied by the investment advisers of banks, mutual funds, insurance companies, pension funds, and brokerage houses. And not only by these professionals, but by an ever growing section of the investing public. The writer has seen hundreds of letters to the publishers of the weekly service **Daily Basis Stock Charts,* in which subscribers tell of market successes that they attribute to their use of the charts. The service itself does not plug any stocks, nor make any recommendations; it just gave the facts (in the form of charts), and these investors felt these facts had given them an added edge in the market.

Charts can't guarantee a winner every time, but here

are some of the things they *can* do:

They can help determine *when* to buy and when to sell, by indicating probable levels of support and resistance, and by signalling trend reversals. . . .

They can call attention—by unusual volume or price behavior—to something happening in an individual company that can be most rewarding. . . .

They help determine the current trend—up, down or sideways—and whether the trend is slowing down or speeding up. . . .

They provide a life history of a stock at a glance, and demonstrate whether one is buying on a rally or on a reaction, and whether the price is historically high or low. . . .

They offer a means for confirming (or rejecting) a decision to buy that is based on economic data or other factors, including stock tips and hunches. . . .

In short, how could we get along without them?

*A stock market chart publication of Trendline.

INDEX

All page numbers in italics refer to terms used in illustrations.

FREE OFFER—The Oldest and Wisest Investment Newsletter in the Newest and Easiest Format

The Outlook is America's oldest continuously published investment advisory newsletter, and now it's available online! Best of all, because you're reading an S&P book, you're entitled to a free 30-day trial. Outlook Online is perfect for both beginners and expert investors alike. The site contains the latest issue of *The Outlook* as well as a searchable archive of the past year's issues. You'll get everything from Standard & Poor's latest individual investment recommendations and economic forecasts to complete portfolios that can help you build wealth. For more than 80 years, *The Outlook* has been identifying the developments that affect stock performance—and making recommendations on when to buy, sell and hold. With Outlook Online you'll also get:

Features on Sectors, Industries and Technical Analysis—These weekly articles will keep you informed about what sectors are poised to outperform, what industries have been on a roll, a where the market may be headed next.

Supervised Master List of Recommended Issues—Standard & Poor's favorites for long-term capital appreciation and superior long-term total return. These groups of stocks have been helping generations of investors build wealth.

Complete Lists of STARS stocks—The highly regarded *Stock Appreciation Ranking System* offers an easy way to pick stocks that Standard & Poor's believes will do best in the near term—six months to one year. Week after week, STARS ranks 1,200 active stocks so you can track changes at a glance.

Platinum and Neural Fair Value Portfolios—Outlook Online also contains detailed information on two more of Standard & Poor's portfolios, both of which have historically outperformed the market by wide margins.

Global Features—Outlook Online is also helpful to investors looking for news and views from abroad. It contains a number of features on both Europe and Asia, including the best picks from S&P's overseas research departments.

Stock and Fund Reports—You'll even get access to 10 free Standard & Poor's reports every month. Whether you're looking for more information on a company or a mutual fund, these reports will help you make informed decisions.

It's simple to activate your free trial to Outlook Online. Just visit the URL below and follow the directions on the screen. No credit card is required and registration will take only a few minutes. To get the best guidance on Wall Street and specific stock recommendations from the experts in the field, just visit us at:

http://www.spoutlookonline.com/ol_mw1.0.asp?ADID=JIL